THE HOSPITAL VISIT

A PASTOR'S GUIDE

Michael L. Kirkindoll

Abingdon Press
Nashville

THE HOSPITAL VISIT
A PASTOR'S GUIDE

Copyright © 2001 by Abingdon Press

This book is printed on recycled, acid-free, elemental-chlorine–free paper.

Library of Congress Cataloging in Publication Data

Kirkindoll, Michael L., 1953–
  The hospital visit: a pastor's guide / Michael L. Kirkindoll.
    p. cm.
  Includes bibliographical references.
  ISBN 0-687-08559-4 (alk. paper)
  1. Church work with the sick. 2. Pastoral medicine. I. Title.

BV4335 K565 2001
259′.411—dc21   00-069998

Scripture quotations noted NIV are from the HOLY BIBLE; NEW INTERNATIONAL VERSION ®. Copyright 1973, 1978, 1984 by International Bible Society. Used by permission of Zondervan Publishing House. All rights reserved.

Scripture quotations noted NLT are from the *Holy Bible*, New Living Translation, copyright © 1996. Used by permission of Tyndale House Publishers, Inc., Wheaton, Illinois 60189. All rights reserved.

Scripture quotations noted *The Message* are from *The Message: The New Testament in Contemporary English*. Copyright © 1993 by Eugene H. Peterson.

The list on pp. 75-76 is from Joint Commission *CAMH 2001 Comprehensive Accreditation Manual for Hospitals*, Examples of Implementation for RI 1 3 5. Oakbrook Terrace, Ill.: Joint Commission on Accreditation of Healthcare Organizations, copyright © 2001, pp. RI-29. Used by permission.

On pp. 73-74 is the Mission Statement of the Pastoral Care Department of the Baptist Health Systems of South Florida (http://www.baptisthealth.net) Used by permission.

01 02 03 04 05 06 07 08 09 10—10 9 8 7 6 5 4 3 2 1

MANUFACTURED IN THE UNITED STATES OF AMERICA

CONTENTS

CHAPTER ONE

Lance's First Visit to the Hospital

Lance had recently begun as our summer youth ministry intern when we went to the hospital for his first pastoral visit. We went to visit Dena, a recent college graduate, who was about Lance's age. She had undergone surgery for a gastrointestinal problem and was anxious to leave the hospital, because she was due to begin medical school in a month. Dena was recovering from her surgery in a timely manner, and we had a pleasant visit. The "fun" started when we were about to leave.

Lance asked permission to pray with Dena. She agreed, and Lance followed the script we had discussed by asking how she wanted us to pray for her. Dena replied by explaining that she couldn't leave until the doctors were certain that there was no intestinal blockage, so she asked us to pray that she would perform a certain biological function that Lance wasn't accustomed to discussing with church folks, much less with God. Lance begged for release from this request with his eyes, which I could not meet because I was afraid that I would laugh out loud. I have no idea what Lance prayed that day (neither does he!), but I do know that he learned quickly that hospital visitation can be exciting.

If you are a parish pastor, or are expecting to become

one some day soon, you will be expected to visit parishioners in the hospital. Your congregation will assume that you already know all there is to know about hospital visitation. You know differently but aren't sure how to learn what to do and when to do it. This chapter will begin to help you learn about hospital visitation by using Rudyard Kipling's "six honest serving-men": Who, What, When, Where, How, and Why.[1]

Who?

Whom will you be visiting in the hospital?

- Members of the congregation and their immediate families.

- Recent visitors to your church who have not yet established a church family.

- A patient in the hospital who requested pastoral care from a pastor in your faith group through the hospital staff.

- Community members, neighbors, friends, and others who may request your presence. You may also be asked to visit friends of congregational members who think a visit would be appropriate. Take these requests seriously, for they constitute a statement of faith in your ministry and are compliments to you.

- Relatives of church members. This can be a problematic area for any pastor. Should you abandon the needs of your faithful members to visit the grandmother of a "once-a-year" attendee of your church? What if the hospital is two hundred miles away? You may be expected to visit the parents of members, but should you be expected to visit aunts, uncles, cousins, neighbors, or friends of members? Do you visit any or all of these in emergency situations? For "major" surgeries? For "routine" surgeries? What are the boundaries of whom you are supposed to visit, and how do these boundaries apply to each individual situation?

These are the real-life questions that can cause misunderstandings and hurt feelings between ministers and congregants. The misunderstandings arise when the minister is not aware of the expectations of the congregation or, even more difficult to know, the expectations of the member and her family. Members may "know" the expectations of the congregation and the customs of the community, while the minister, an outsider, has no sense of what is considered proper and appropriate.

Hurt feelings result when the pastor knowingly, or even unknowingly, fails to meet the unwritten expectations of the congregation and thereby offends the patient or his family by "ignoring" them and their needs. Is it possible to avoid these conflicts?

Unfortunately, the pastor will never be able to meet all the expectations of the congregation and its members. You will never be able to avoid these conflicts because you will never have all the information, time, and energy that you need. A highly respected pastor described hospital visitation, though, as "paying the rent." It is wise to manage your time and make the effort to visit the hospital appropriately.

How can you be proactive in minimizing conflict over hospital visitation? Schedule time to discuss these issues with the pastor-parish relations committee or personnel committee of your congregation. Educate them on the potential for misunderstanding. Ask them to provide guidelines for you to follow. Demonstrate your willingness to make pastoral visits by "paying the rent." Seek help from other clergy staff or lay leadership when the load becomes burdensome. Protect your time away from church responsibilities by enlisting the help of others. Make friends with the chaplaincy staff at your local hospitals and trust them to help you. In these ways you will balance the responsibilities of hospital visitation and fulfill your call to minister to the sick.

What?

What circumstances will require you to travel to the hospital to make a pastoral visit? Surgery is the most common reason. You may visit before the surgery, after the surgery to find out if the patient and family are in satisfactory condition, and during the postoperative recovery period. Each of these visits will possibly relate to surgery, but each is unique. There may be anxiety before and during the surgery, relief if the surgery is successful and grief if it is not, and uncertainty about the future after the surgery. You should be attentive to the signs of these emotions and help the family to confront each emotion in turn. Avoid trying to "fix" these feelings that the family may have, for their feelings are a natural outcome of the experience of surgery.

With the ascent of managed care, you will increasingly confront "day surgeries." It is important to learn the location of the "day surgery suite" or the "short-term operations" waiting room. The patients who undergo such procedures will not enter the hospital until just before their procedure, and will be released as soon as the recovery period has ended. You will be fortunate to be able to see the patient at all and will more likely be able to minister only to the family. Occasionally you may be able to see the patient if they are waiting for the procedure to begin, or even more rarely, be allowed to visit the patient during recovery. Short visits are obviously best here, and *encouragement* is the key word for the patient and family.

Maternity visits are emotionally loaded experiences. If all has gone well, there is no happier time to share with your parishioner. Be sensitive, however, to the new parents. Though the baby may be the star of the show, the parents need the attention most, and may have anxieties about their adequacy as parents. They will almost certainly be exhausted from the experience and will need to rest before taking the baby home. If the birth has had complications, then you will want to share all the love and support that you can with the parents and family. Your presence, concern, and prayers will provide the spiritual foundation necessary to help them to find their own way through their difficulties.

Emergency calls are particularly difficult for pastors. The family may be in shock or in denial, they may be blaming themselves or blaming the injured person for their misery, or they may act as if nothing has happened. You can convey through your presence the support of the congregation. You may seek the help of the hospital chaplain to know what is going on in the emergency room. You might run errands or make phone calls for the family. You might bring them food or something to drink to make them more comfortable. You can be there when you are needed to give spiritual comfort. There are no simple rules for ministering in an emergency situation, so rely on your sense of God's guidance, prayer, and the hospital chaplain, who has been trained to respond to emergencies and is more experienced than you are in this area.

You will also visit retirement homes, assisted-living centers, and nursing homes. The time you spend with the patient is an offering of love, and will be appreciated by the patient and the family. At their best, these are facilities that provide the care needed to enable a person to enjoy living without the worry of a home to care for. At their worst, such facilities lend themselves to dehumanizing the patient because of the structure necessary to operate them. In either case, the pastor can offer a valuable gift to the patient by spending time and showing concern. These visits can be the most rewarding that a minister can make, for senior citizens reward their ministers with love and support.

When?

When is a pastor supposed to visit a parishioner in the hospital? The most common times are:

- Before and after surgery
- When a child is born
- During a medical illness
- When death is imminent
- During and after an emergency
- When mental health treatment is needed

Not all members of your congregation will welcome your visit during a hospital stay. Some members wish to keep their hospital stays private for personal reasons. Some do not wish to be visited because they are embarrassed by the nature of their condition. Some no longer think of their faith as relevant to their medical condition, or are mad at the church for some reason. Some simply forget to notify the church that they are entering the hospital. While you may not know why you have not been requested to visit the person, you can always ask permission: "May I visit with you for a moment while you are in the hospital?" Asking this question will protect you from the complaint later that you did not visit the member.

Do respect the visiting hours of the hospital unless

you have no other option, and then ask for permission from the nursing staff to visit in the room. This is particularly important if you wish to visit a parishioner of the opposite sex. Always place the privacy and wishes of the patient as your highest priority, and you will rarely have to apologize for your actions. When in doubt, ask!

One of the most troubling situations for pastors is finding out too late that a parishioner has been in the hospital and has already returned home. Sometimes a friend or family member agrees to notify the pastor of an upcoming hospital stay and forgets to make the necessary contact. Sometimes a message taken for the pastor then is misplaced or forgotten. Sometimes a family will assume that someone else will tell the pastor about the hospital stay. Occasionally, a simple miscommunication leads to misunderstanding. When a pastor finds out about a hospital stay after it is completed, it is already too late. He or she will probably learn about the problem from a disgruntled parishioner who uses the situation to "make a point." The only constructive way of handling such a conflict is to seek out the aggrieved party and to explain the situation. If you are in the wrong, apologize and take responsibility for your actions. If not, ask who contacted the church and when the contact was made. Behave in a positive and loving manner, and maintain a professional demeanor, but communicate the full circumstances of the occurrence to the unhappy person. Share a report on the event with the appropriate lay committee and ask for help in avoiding future conflicts. Some experiences in the ministry just are not fun!

Where?

Most of your pastoral care visits will be made at the hospitals that serve your area. Whenever you visit a particular hospital for the first time, it is both courteous and wise to visit the chaplain's office. You can either visit with a member of the chaplaincy staff, or schedule an appointment for such a visit. Often the chaplain's office will issue you a "clergy badge" or some other identification specifying your relationship to your parishioners. These are helpful for you, as well as for the hospital staff, and will make your ministry more effective by allowing more freedom in your visitation. The chaplain's office will also explain to you procedures for parking your vehicle. Most hospitals provide complimentary parking for pastors, and may provide designated parking places for clergy. Since you will make many visits in hospitals, it is good stewardship of time and finance to understand how each hospital functions in these areas.

Visits to some units of the hospital require a different approach. The Intensive Care (ICU), Cardiac Care (CCU), Cardiac Intensive Care (CICU), Surgical Intensive Care (SICU), Pediatric Intensive Care (PICU), and Neonatal Intensive Care (NICU) are all units of the hospital that must have more stringent visitation requirements for health reasons. Usually there is an intercom system by which you can contact someone at the nursing station who will explain visiting procedures to you. Generally, ministers are allowed to make visits to parishioners at times other than those reserved for family in such units, but this is not always true. By acting in a professional and courteous manner at these units, you can earn the respect of the hospital staff and usually become more effective in providing care for the family.

Some hospitals use volunteers to provide information about the families present in the waiting rooms of these units. This is particularly helpful when you do not recognize anyone in the waiting room. These volunteers can often find the family you came to visit, and can help you follow the appropriate procedures.

You should also be particularly sensitive to appropriate behaviors in the maternity area of the hospital. Follow visiting hours strictly, and ask for directions for entering any room of this wing. The nurses or staff can help you to avoid embarrassing yourself or others!

Contact a mental health facility before making a visit. You will probably need to be on a list of visitors approved by the patient or family before you are allowed to make a visit. Such facilities are responsible to their patients to provide a higher level of patient confidentiality, so you may be asked to sign a form stating that you will not disclose what you discuss with a patient with others. This is standard procedure for mental health providers. When you make such a visit, be yourself, prepare yourself spiritually for God's guidance in your visit, and ask for help from the staff if you have any questions about your visit.

How?

How do you make a visit to a parishioner in the hospital? A typical pastoral visit would include the following:

- entering the room (not always as easy as it sounds!)
- greeting the patient and others
- inquiring about the patient's condition
- offering support and comfort
- praying and /or reading Scripture with the patient
- exiting the room

Before you enter a hospital room, be aware of not taking unwanted germs with you. Wash your hands and brush your teeth before you go to the hospital. Avoid wearing perfume or cologne since some people are allergic to them. Present a professional appearance, but in most areas it is no longer necessary to dress in strict "business" style. "Business casual" may actually relax your parishioner—after all, would you dress casually if you expected them to die?

Knock as softly as possible for the patient to hear—you do not want to wake the patient if she is asleep. If you receive an invitation, enter the room carefully, but if not, it is permissible to open the door just far enough to see if anyone is with the patient. Never enter a room without permission if the patient is undergoing any kind of care. If the patient is asleep, check to see if anyone is sitting with the patient. Talk to this person in the hall, if possible, to avoiding waking the patient.

When you enter the room, introduce yourself immediately to anyone whom you do not already know. Do not make someone ask your name! If you have a business card, and you should always carry at least one business card for each patient that you are going to visit, offer it to a caregiver whom you do not know.

Speak first to the patient, then to the others in the room. An example of an "icebreaker" is: "Hello, my name is Mickey Kirkindoll. I am the pastor of Jefferson First Baptist Church, and I wanted to visit you. I hope you are feeling well today." The response that follows will usually tell you what you wish to know about the patient.

What if you do not know why the patient is in the hospital? It is permissible and even wise, to ask permission to gain this information. Ask, "Would you mind sharing with me why you are in the hospital?" Use the same words to discuss the patient's condition as he or she uses with you: "I'm having tummy troubles" is not specific, but may be all that the patient wishes to tell you. "I have cancer" or "I had a mastectomy" is more specific and gives you permission to discuss the patient's condition further.

Sometimes you may visit a patient who is "unresponsive"—in a coma, sedated, or incapacited by having had a stroke. Talk to the patient also, for there is evidence that a person in such a condition may hear you. Don't just talk about the patient, talk to the patient and pray with the patient.

How long should you stay at the hospital with a patient or family? Generally, families seem to appreciate shorter visits than twenty years ago. Stay long enough to convey your concern, but not so long as to be a burden on the family. They may have things to discuss without you, or may feel a burden to entertain you, so be sensitive to their needs. Remember that this visit is about the patient and family, not about you.

When you feel that it is time to leave, say something like "Before I go, may I pray with you?" This allows you to use the prayer to bring closure to your visit. Ask, "How may I pray for you today?" In so doing, you will convey your desire to offer spiritual support and still respect the privacy of the patient and family. The appendix to this book offers bedside prayers from male and female clergy of several denominations, if your faith tradition does not require the use of a prayer book.

Why?

Wayne Oates, a noted author and pastoral counselor, told this story: After pastoring for the first six years of his ministry, he became the chaplain of a general hospital. One afternoon he was called to the bedside of a male patient. The patient greeted Oates with a direct question: "Be you the man of God in this hospital?" After a pause, Oates replied: "Yes, sir, I am the man of God in this hospital." The patient then retold the story of the ax head in 2 Kings 6, and said: "Well, the ax has done flown off the handle for me. I've never been sick a day in my life, but now they tell me I got cancer of the bowels. They are gonna cut on me tomorrow. So, I sent for you! Can you help me?"

Each pastor is the "man or woman of God" in such a situation. Your personal understanding of your role as minister and your relationship with God will determine how, and in what sense, you will be able to relate to others as a person in whom the presence of God resides. Here is how Wayne Oates answered for himself the man's question: "Suddenly, I realized that neither he nor I was alone. God was with us. Though the body of this man was in jeopardy, the Eternal was his Sustainer. I was a message of that Presence in visitation."[2]

Nothing that a pastor does involves her or him as directly in the lives of parishioners as hospital visitation. A caring pastor who is sensitive, respectful, and competent in hospital visitation is a blessing to any patient, family, or congregation. Hospital visitation can be for the pastor a legacy of "little, nameless, unremembered acts of kindness and of love."[3]

Notes

1. Rudyard Kipling, "The Elephant's Child," in *Just So Stories*, (New York: Signet Classics, 1974), p. 56.

2. Wayne E. Oates, *The Presence of God in Pastoral Counseling* (Waco, Tex.: Word, 1986), pp. 28-29.

3. William Wordsworth, "Lines Composed a Few Miles Above Tintern Abbey," lines 33-35, in *Complete Poetical Works*, Thomas Hutchinson, ed. Revised by Ernest de Selincourt. (Oxford: Oxford Univ. Press, 1936), p. 164.

CHAPTER TWO

The Pastor as Christ:
Relating to the Patient

Mrs. Burns, age eighty-four, is in the hospital for the third time in six months, in this instance for liver failure secondary to cancer. She is suffering almost constant pain, and is exhausted physically, emotionally, and spiritually from battling her disease. She is one of the "pillars of her church," with a long history of service to others and support for her congregation of believers.

"I want to die. I am ready to die. I am not afraid to die." With the fortitude earned by years of living, she is facing her death and facing her pastor. It is now your turn to speak. What will you say, how will you act, how will you pray with her?

Every pastor has been or will be in this situation. The purpose of this chapter is to suggest a theological basis for this kind of pastoral care, to help you understand what it is like to be a hospital patient, to provide you with resources you can utilize in becoming an effective hospital visitor, and to prepare you for some of the situations you may face.

The Pastor as Christ

Matthew's Gospel contains this story from the ministry of Jesus: "Jesus went through all the towns and villages, teaching in their synagogues, preaching the good news of the kingdom and healing every disease and sickness. When he saw the crowds, he had compassion on them, because they were harassed and helpless, like sheep without a shepherd" (Matt. 9:35-36 NIV). Each of the Gospel writers comments on the compassion of Jesus, and each mention of his compassion for the people is followed by an action or command from Jesus that will bring relief to the people. The "sheep and goats" judgment described in Matthew's Gospel records the priority that Jesus placed on compassion-motivated ministry: If a person does not actively seek to minister to those who are ill, he stands judged as unworthy of heaven. The point of this is clear to each of us involved in pastoral care: We are to minister to the sick with the same compassion that Jesus has for us.

What does it mean to have compassion for someone else? From a theological point of view, we are to share the burdens of others as Christ shared our burdens (Phil. 2:5-11). From a practical point of view with regard to hospital visitation, compassion can be characterized by four "be-attitudes":

Be there when you are needed.
Be accepting of the actions and feelings of the patient.
Bear the sufferings of the patient as a gift of love.
Bring a message of hope.

Be Present

"Your being here means more than you will ever know." These are some of the sweetest words a pastor can ever hear. Your presence is a reminder that the patient is a member of a church family, and that Christ himself is present in the life of each of his sisters and brothers. You may not feel like it, look like it, or act like it, but your presence at the hospital bedside is a visible reminder of God's care for the patient, and it is much easier to see you than to be aware of God's presence. Job's three friends, who got it wrong so much of the time, got it right at the start: They came and sat with Job for seven days and seven nights without saying a word (Job 2:11-13).

Even with all of the recent advancements in communications technology, it is still essential for a pastor to train her congregation to contact her whenever there is an illness in the church family. I have made several suggestions in the first chapter on how to avoid and reconcile miscommunications about a hospital stay, but this is too important an issue not to repeat this encouragement—ask the members of the congregation to contact you whenever they know of a hospitalization. It is better to receive the same message ten times than never to receive the message at all. Remind the members of the congregation to call you, and not to assume that the family did so—we all know where that leads!

Be Accepting

When a person is in physical, mental, or spiritual distress, he may say or do things that he does not mean and would normally not do. When you visit a person in the hospital, your primary purpose is to comfort and support the patient and family, not to pass judgment or correct theology. Allow and encourage the patient to express feelings of anger, despair, or hostility, and remember the grace with which God listens to you.

The most intriguing aspect for me of the story of the men who sought to trap Jesus by "setting up" a woman in order to use her as a public example is the grace-filled manner in which Jesus treats her. He drives away her accusers with his words to give her a moment alone with him, and so that her exit might be more dignified than her entrance. Jesus looks at her and says, "If the others will not accuse you, neither will I. You can leave now, but leave behind your sin as well." Without condoning her sin, he conveyed a love and acceptance for her that we would do well to emulate.

Bear the Suffering of Others

Hospitals can be happy places, but far more often you will be called on to witness the suffering of others. Sometimes you will even be accosted and commanded to instruct God to end the patient's suffering. As the resident theologian and "holy person," you may be asked to explain why God allows suffering in this world. Your inclination will be to want to do something for the sufferer to fix the problem, or to defend God. Resist this inclination. The greatest gift that you, as a minister, can offer a suffering person or her family is to take her and her suffering seriously, to bear her burden in prayer, and to leave healing up to God. Eugene Peterson, in his eloquent and wise book *Five Smooth Stones for Pastoral Work*, offers this prescription for dealing with suffering: "Nothing, in the long run, does more to demean the person who suffers than to condescendingly busy oneself in fixing him or her up, and nothing can provide more meaning to suffering than a resolute and quiet faithfulness in taking the suffering seriously and offering a companionship through the time of waiting for the morning."[1]

Bring Hope

In contradiction to much of what is written, our faith is centered on hope, not despair; on faith, not certitude; and on the present, not the future. The New Testament writers wrote of hope three times more often than suffering. The pastoral visitor to the hospital brings with him the same emphasis on hope. His presence is, again, a sign of hope, for he reminds the patient of a praying congregation and the hope that their prayers will be answered. As one friend said in comforting my wife during a difficult time in our lives: "You just live right now. The rest of us will be praying for you." At a time when prayer was particularly difficult, these were sweet words indeed.

What kind of hope do you have to offer others? The faith of the Christian has a specific source in God the Father, Christ the Son, and the Holy Spirit (Rom. 5:1-5; 15:13; 1 Pet. 1:3-5). The Christian can trust in the power of hope because it is promised by Scripture (Rom. 15:4), delivered through a new birth of the Spirit (1 Pet. 1:3), and poured out in our hearts through the power of the Holy Spirit (Rom. 5:4-5). Faith in God gives life to our hope (Rom. 8:24-25), and is the substantiation of our hope (Heb. 11:1). Christian faith has content: (1) that we will be delivered by God (2 Cor. 1:10); (2) that we will receive the grace of God as well as eternal life (2 Thess. 2:16; Titus 1:2); and (3) that our hope will produce endurance in our hearts (1 Thess. 1:3).

Illness as a Separation

The person who is hospitalized is in a particularly vulnerable situation. The minister who seeks to be sensitive to these anxieties will be of great comfort to her. From the admissions process to the taking away of her clothes in exchange for a hospital gown, the patient may feel dehumanized by the entire process. She has become numbers on a wristband and a "case" to be diagnosed and healed, generally with little say-so in the process. Though hospitals work diligently to reduce the anxieties and dehumanization of the process, most likely the patient will experience hospitalization as a time of separation.

Separation from One's Identity

When Mrs. Burns entered the hospital, an admissions counselor placed a wristband on her nonwriting arm. With the exception of her nurses, few of those who care for Mrs. Burns will call her by name, but they will all verify her identity by her wristband. While hospitals are busy places, and the proper identification of the patient is obviously of paramount importance, Mrs. Burns will soon recognize that her identity exists chiefly on her arm. She will not be recognized for her wonderful pound cake or winning smile, or even for being a devoted grandmother and great-grandmother. This is where a compassionate minister can be especially helpful. You know her family, and her stories, and her reputation. Call her by name, find out how her family is doing, talk to her about her feelings, and you will have ministered to her effectively and kindly.

Separation from One's Autonomy

Until this point in her life, Mrs. Burns has largely been able to look after herself. Perhaps the only other times she has been in the hospital were for the births of her children, so she is used to making most of her own decisions about her daily activities. Not so in the hospital, for she will need to conform to the hospital schedule. She doesn't wish to appear unreasonable and complaining, even though she is not resting as much as usual, and someone is likely to come into her room at the most inconvenient times. Her life is in the hands of others, and this brings with it unwelcome reminders of being treated as a child. As her pastor you can treat her with respect, and always, always, be aware of not offending her modesty. A compassionate pastor will, by mode of address and behavior, remind Mrs. Burns that she has had a life outside the confines of the hospital and is someone worthy of respect.

Separation from Community

Life in the hospital is boring for Mrs. Burns. She misses her house, her church, her hairdresser, her grocery store, her friends. All there is to do is watch television, and she is used to "puttering around" her house and talking on the telephone to her friends. Her friends come to see her sometimes, but they seem to feel uncomfortable in her hospital room and stay either too long or not long enough. Then again, someone always seems to be interrupting her conversations. She is particularly lonely on Sunday mornings and Wednesday evenings, or at the other times when her "gang" gets together. She feels all alone and wants to go back home, to her friends and church. Her pastor reminds her of her church and her friends and knows the things she wants to know about her world. A pastor who cares enough to spend time with her, and loves her even though her hair hasn't been styled in a week, will bring joy to her life and the reminder that she does have a family of faith that cares for her.

Separation from Defenses

It seems that all Mrs. Burns can do is think. She misses all the things that used to keep her busy, and now, with nothing else to occupy her thoughts, all she seems to do is think about dying. She has known all along that she would die someday, and she is afraid that someday may be soon. She worries about the cost of the hospital stay, and whether or not she will be able to afford it. She worries about the impact of her illness on her family. She feels separated from reality, because she seems trapped by her room and the sameness of every day. On the other hand, at moments it seems that reality is more than she really wants to handle. She wonders if God knows how she feels, and if so, why doesn't God do something about it? *The odd thing is*, she thinks, *I never used to worry about things like this.*

As her pastor, you may not be able to give her all the reassurance that she needs, but you can read Scripture with her, and pray with her, and sit by her side. Your presence is a reminder of her former life and a gentle tug back toward reality. You are there with her, and that is what she needs the most.

Resources for Relating

There has been a great deal of discussion in the area of hospital visitation that the minister is part of a "patient care team" or "healing team." Though I am no expert in these matters, in my experience the concept of "team" has been more theoretical than practical, because the presuppositions, goals, and skills of the minister are vastly different from those of medical personnel. The minister's concern is for the whole person—body, mind, and spirit—and her tools for healing are spiritual tools. If you substitute "practice medicine" in the place of "wage war," and "tools" in the place of "weapons," the assertions of 2 Corinthians 10:3-4 ring true: "For though we live in the world, we do not wage war as the world does. The weapons we fight with are not the weapons of the world. On the contrary, they have divine power to demolish strongholds" (NIV). As ministers, we have access to resources different from those of modern medicine, but our resources are even more powerful than those of medical personnel. We should neither downplay our role in the healing ministry nor exchange the resources that are distinctly ours for those of medical therapeutics. Instead, we should hone the skills that are ours for the benefit of the patient.

Listening

Effective listening is both a skill and a discipline. It requires that the practitioner be wholly present to the patient in a way that is unnatural for most of us. Being present to the patient is our spiritual priority, and Jesus himself is our example. It is remarkable that he is always depicted as completely engaged when he is present with others. This is a skill that, with experience and discipline, we, too, can learn. A full-scale treatment of listening skills is well beyond the scope of this book; consider reading *Listening and Caring Skills* by John Savage (Abingdon Press, 1996). This is a highly readable and yet complete summary of how to become a skilled listener. The following brief treatment of listening skills owes much to this book.

Use questions to discover the patient's feelings and meanings. Skillful questioning builds a bridge between the speaker and the listener. A seemingly simple question like "How are you?" is an invitation to the hearer to unload burdens to the listener and to unlock secrets that have become burdensome. Listen carefully to the speaker, and follow his lead by using follow-up questions that lead him to a greater degree of self-disclosure. Use questions like "What else . . ." and "How long . . ." to keep the conversation going. Tailor your questions to the speaker's previous response in a thoughtful way, and you will gain much of the information you need for effective ministry. Avoid questions that begin with "why" unless the object of your question is simply to gain information. For many people, the word *why* is a blaming word, and the speaker will likely end meaningful conversation when he does not feel accepted by the listener.

Listen as well for undisclosed meaning in a statement. The patient may not wish to appear to be negative and may therefore delete information from his response to your question, hoping that you will be able to "listen between the lines" and discern the additional meaning of his response. This technique is particularly valuable in listening to the stories a patient often tells you about some past event. Be on the alert for "back then . . . but now" statements that may tell you about the speaker's present insecurities or fears.

Be sensitive to hearing clues that your visit has reached its end. Many people will not wish to offend a minister and so will not communicate directly a need for more rest or space. "Leave them wanting more" is a show-business adage that also works well for ministers.

Paraphrase your response to ensure clear communication. Paraphrasing is the "act of saying back to the speaker in your own words what you heard the speaker say."[2] The purpose of paraphrasing is to narrow the possibility that the listener has incorrectly understood the intent of the speaker. Paraphrasing is done by reducing the statement by the speaker to its key words, and adding a "stem" to indicate to the speaker that you are attempting to give a reasonable response to her statement. A "stem" is introductory language that gives the hearer time to formulate a response. Common stems are:

- "You are saying that . . ."
- "I hear you saying that . . ."
- "What I hear you telling me is . . ."
- "If I hear you right, you are telling me that . . ."

Let us test this concept. Suppose you are visiting in a hospital room and your parishioner says: "I'm so upset that I cannot even sleep. This cancer's gotten hold of me and I can't seem to shake it. The doctor said that he was going to do more tests, but we all know what that means. It's a known fact that they never tell you what you need to know. Who am I kidding? I've bought the farm."

Start by breaking down what you have just heard into its key components. The speaker is upset. The doctor visited, and the patient assumed from his statement that since he was going to do more tests, that her condition is terminal. The patient is understandably upset by her conclusion.

Choose a stem to begin your response, then repeat the key words of her statement in your response: *"What I hear you saying is* that your *doctor* told you he wanted to do *more tests* and you are *afraid* that *he means* you are *dying."*

The practice of paraphrasing is not difficult when you are reading these words, but when you are listening and the patient is speaking rapidly or indistinctly, it requires intense concentration and experience to be effective. It is, however, a worthwhile expenditure of your time and a valuable skill to be learned.

Use a "perception check" to identify the emotions behind a speaker's words. Often a speaker will attempt consciously or unconsciously to convey her emotional condition without actually naming an emotion. This is often true in a hospital setting, particularly when the pastor does not know the patient well. Using a "perception check" allows the pastor to guess at the emotions felt by the speaker, and to open a door to ministry by using a non-threatening communication technique.

Consider the example above. The first step is to observe the body language of the speaker. Begin by looking at her face. Is her face flushed? Do you see bulging veins or a tense look on her face? Is she, or has she been crying? Are her arms crossed or is she wrapping her arms around her chest? Are her hands clenched? Is she drumming her fingers or rocking her legs or feet? Is she avoiding eye contact or pleading with you with unblinking eyes? Through years of socialization you will have learned to interpret many of these clues, but be aware that research suggests that each gender is more adept at reading the clues of its own gender, and more likely to misinterpret the emotions of the other.

How did the speaker's voice sound? Was it higher or

lower than normal? Was it raspy, breathy, or more rapid than usual? Does it reveal sadness, happiness, fear, or joy? Did it seem constricted and robot-like? From these and other clues, you will have another basis on which to guess about the emotional condition of the speaker.

From these nonverbal clues as well as from the verbal communication that you received, you are now ready to hazard a guess about the speaker's emotional condition. Name that emotion to yourself. Is she sad, angry, afraid? Then reflect on your relationship with the speaker. Do you know her well? Do you have a high or low level of trust in your relationship? This issue is important, because it is much better to reduce the emotional content of your response than to overstate it when you are dealing with a person with whom you do not have a high level of trust.

Now you are ready to respond. The quaver in the speaker's voice, the high pitch of her voice, her "wrapped up" body language and her use of euphemisms for death all seem to point to the same conclusion: The patient is extremely afraid of dying. How do you formulate a verbal response? Begin with a stem such as:

- "It seems to me that you might be feeling . . ."
- "I get the impression that . . ."
- "I have the sense that . . ."
- "Would I be on the right track if I said that you might be feeling . . ."

Next add the appropriate emotional description to the statement. "Boy, you sure are scared to death," would be callous, wouldn't it? So reduce the intensity of your statement appropriately: "It seems to me that you are feeling a little scared by the doctor's visit." Note that you have added a context to your statement—"by the doctor's visit." This particularizes your response. Now follow up your statement by asking if you have perceived her emotional state correctly, and you have the full perception check: "It seems to me that you are feeling a little scared by the doctor's visit. Is that true?" Some experts suggest that you might use the question "Am I right?" in this situation, but I avoid it because it might seem to place the emphasis on my skill rather than on the speaker's emotions. I have also found that it seems effective to ask, "Is that about right?" or "Is that in the right ballpark?" The latter works particularly well with men, for it places your question in the parlance of sports, which is usually a safe area of conversation.

Despite the fact that this seems to be a lengthy process, you will do much of this work instinctually. The purpose of training yourself to do it thoughtfully is to make yourself more sensitive to others, and thereby a more effective minister.

Be aware, also, that the speaker is evaluating your nonverbal communication and reaching conclusions about your feelings. The best way to handle this is to be yourself, and to trust God to help you remain open, honest, and faith-full no matter how stressful the situation. Compassion will project from your behavior if you are prepared to offer it to others.

Using Scripture

Some pastors always read from the Scriptures during a hospital visit. Some never seem to read from the Scriptures, preferring instead to emphasize the relational aspects of their hospital ministry. Some denominations have prayer books that prescribe certain verses for the situations a minister may encounter at the hospital bedside, and some denominations do not. Whether, and how, you use Scripture in hospital ministry will depend on these and other considerations, but one observation is warranted: When appropriately used, there is no greater tool at the minister's disposal for bringing comfort to the patient.

The immediate question to face is which passage of Scripture to use. My belief is that every pastor should develop for herself or himself an inventory of Scripture passages for hospital use and memorize them. You will not always have a Bible at hand, and there is comfort in knowing that you are prepared for the unknown. In some versions of the Bible, a thoughtful editor has included a list of scriptures to be used when the reader is in a particular mood or facing a particular situation. There is nothing wrong with using this list, but, for me at least, using this sort of resource smacks of magic. On the other hand, Bible reading can be used appropriately in a prescriptive manner, particularly if the patient requests it. "I seem to be lacking hope," you hear your parishioner say. It is then entirely appropriate to read aloud one of the many passages from the Scripture that affirm our hope in God.

Which version of the Bible should you read? The simplest answer to that question is whichever you own and are most comfortable reading. Any, or every, version of the Scriptures has something to say for it and someone for whom it is appropriate. Use your own good judgment and sanctified common sense, and you will stay on the solid ground of God's Word. There is, however, one exception to this principle in my experience: People overwhelmingly want to hear the Psalms in the King James Version. The beauty of the language and its familiarity, especially in the Twenty-third Psalm, make the KJV clearly preferred in this area.

From a practical perspective, many older people in the hospital will not have the use of their hearing aids. You may have to read more loudly than usual and pay particular care to your enunciation. Remember to use an appropriate volume level if the patient is in a semiprivate room. Read with emotional expression, and allow the scripture to have its maximum emotional impact. Consider using a daily devotional guide to direct your Scripture reading. The *Upper Room* is an excellent product that is widely used in different denominations. Ask for permission to leave it for the patient to read. One warning: It is never appropriate to go from room to room in the hospital and leave religious literature without asking permission. This is much more likely to do harm than good.

Celebrating Communion

Is there a more powerful or effective resource in ministering to the chronically or terminally ill than that of Holy Communion? For me, the answer is an emphatic no, but I came to this understanding after I had been in the ministry for a while. As a lifelong Baptist, I wasn't even aware that such a thing was possible, and, indeed, there are Baptists and others of good faith who oppose such a "nonchurch" use of the Lord's Supper. In other denominations, it is permissible for lay ministers to administer the elements, providing that they have been properly consecrated.

What is most appropriate, it seems to me, is to know the custom of your own faith tradition and abide by it in good faith. The celebration of the Eucharist has long separated Christians, so let us agree to respect the convictions of others, as well as our own, and use the communion service as appropriate for our parishioners. For those of you who have never celebrated communion in the hospital, let me encourage you to try it if it is appropriate. I have found it to be a moving and affirming experience for the patient. Do be sure to ask the nurse for permission to do so, and ask for privacy for the service as well, so that it might be done in a dignified manner.

Praying

When, how, and what do you pray at the hospital bed-side?

For some pastors, the prayer at bedside is prescribed by custom and usage, and so the choices that other pastors must face are unnecessary. Other pastors have no guidelines of any sort, and so guidance particularly is needed. I have long followed a practice of having prayer not long before I leave the room, though there are fine pastors who object to such a practice as deni-grating the importance of prayer. It is wise to ask per-mission before you have prayer. I usually ask as well: "How may I pray for you today?" or "How would you like for me to pray for you today?" This question allows the patient to voice particular concerns. If I know the patient well, I may ask the patient if she would like to pray with me, and afterward I usually close the prayer. I stand beside the bed where the patient can see me, and I hold her hand if that is appro-priate. I try to touch the patient if at all possible, with either the shoulder or the arm as second choices to the hand. I try to include family members, if present, in the prayer circle as well as mentioning them by name in the prayer itself. I pray for divine skill for the doctors and nurses who attend the patient, and ask for rest, com-fort, and peace for the patient. In the appendix to this book, I have included a number of bedside prayers for your use.

What about praying for healing? Is this always appro-priate? While it seems appropriate to me to ask God for healing (God can, and does, do miracles), it also seems better to me to ask what is God's will, and to give to the patient and family the grace to accept the outcome, whatever it may be. It is also appropriate, in the proper context, to ask God to give the sufferer a meaningful death. What is inappropriate, in my opinion, is the need felt by some pastors to "name and claim" healing with no reference to the will of God.

My sister-in-law, Renae Hester, is an ordained chaplain and minister. In one instance, she was called to a hospital room in her role as chaplain to minister to the family of a terminally ill child. While she was with the family, a young pastor came into the room, prayed, announced that the child was healed and would soon be well again, and then left. All of this took place within the space of five minutes. No sooner had he left the room than the child went into cardiac arrest and died, leaving Reverend Hester to deal with a distraught and confused family. This sort of ignorance and arrogance has no place in ministry. Fortunately, it is a fairly rare experience.

Resources for Special Situations

Developing effective hospital visitation skills, along with the grace of God, will enable you to minister in any situation in which you find yourself. There are some situations, however, that call for special guidelines.

Visiting a Patient Who Has Just Signed "Informed Consent" Forms

You may well find a person who is in emotional shock. The decision to come to the hospital may have come easily, or as a necessity, but the impact of reading that long list of possible outcomes from being in the hospital or undergoing surgery will daunt even the most level-headed person. I have frequently seen patients and their families in tears or on the verge of leaving the hospital after such an experience. What can you do? Point out that such forms are required by law and include a great many outcomes, which are statistically very unlikely to occur. Remind the patient and family that the nature of our litigious society compels doctors and hospitals to protect themselves against spurious lawsuits. Gently assert the obvious: God is still in command of the situation, and God's care is the only sure foundation on which to trust.

Visiting Restricted Units

There are units of the hospital that have restricted visitation times for good reason. Being a pastor does not give you the authority to ignore those restrictions. Frequently, though, if you are respectful of the patient's privacy and need for rest, as well as the medical staff's duty to provide care, you can visit the patient at times other than those authorized for the general public. Generally, there is an intercom button or telephone you can use to contact the medical staff. State your name and relationship to the patient, ask for permission to make a brief visit, and abide by the answer. If you are respectful when denied access or asked to wait until a later time, you will establish a positive relationship with the hospital staff.

Visiting a Patient Who Cannot Speak

At some time you may visit a patient who is in a coma, has had a stroke, or has a tube down his throat and thus cannot communicate. In this case, address the patient directly and lovingly, avoid asking questions that call for a response, pray for the patient and family, and be brief, unless it is appropriate for you to visit with any family members staying with the patient. Patients who are not able to speak are also frequently incontinent, so be aware that hospital visitation is not always pleasant, and your purpose is to bring comfort to others, not to yourself. Carry out your visit with all the grace that you can.

Visiting a Patient in a Psychiatric Hospital

Always call at least one day in advance and ask for information about the restrictions on visitation. Keep in mind that such facilities place a high value on confidentiality, and you will not be allowed to speak to your parishioner without prior approval. Many facilities require that the patient or family give permission for you to visit or talk with the patient, and you may not have been included. If not, and if such a visit seems appropriate, contact the family and ask them to handle the situation. Remember your role in such a facility: You are there to bring spiritual comfort, not to practice counseling or medicine. If you have questions about what is appropriate in your situation, ask the medical staff. They will be glad to guide you.

Notes

1. Eugene Peterson, *Five Smooth Stones for Pastoral Work* (Grand Rapids: Eerdmans, 1992), p. 141.

2. John Savage, *Listening and Caring Skills in Ministry: A Guide for Pastors, Counselors, and Small Groups* (Nashville: Abingdon Press, 1996), p. 23.

CHAPTER THREE

The Pastor as Holy Spirit: Relating to the Spouse and Family

Mr. Riley is an elderly man, hospitalized with multiple complications from cancer. He knows that he is dying, and he talks incessantly about his early life. He repeatedly asserts that he has had a good life and that he has done the best that he could. Riley knows that he was an inattentive and emotionally distant parent, and that his children suffered long-term psychological scars from his parenting deficiencies. His family and the family of his second wife are in the ICU waiting room, where the atmosphere is emotionally charged. There have been tensions between them, principally over the inheritance that he is expected to leave. There is little conversation between Riley's children, and even less between them and the "other" family. You enter the waiting room and introduce yourself: "Hello, I'm Mickey Kirkindoll, Mr. Riley's pastor. May I visit with you briefly?"

This is not an unusual scenario. Neither would it be unusual if such a visit were preceded by visits to a new mother and to a parishioner recovering from surgery, both of whom have required a significant expenditure of spiritual and emotional energy. Now you face a smorgasbord of emotional trauma, family dysfunction, personal antagonism, and spiritual confusion, with a healthy dose of disordered communication included.

Not even a psychiatrist would relish the situation in which you find yourself, but there is no backing out. What will you do and say to these hurting people?

The Role of the Holy Spirit in the Pastor's Ministry

Take heart, Pastor, you are not alone! Your companion and guide is the Holy Spirit, who is given to you by Christ to strengthen you and make you effective in your ministry. By yourself, you might be lost, but empowered by the Spirit, you are adequate for this situation. How will the Spirit help you?

- By dwelling in you. (John 14:16-17)
- By helping you know what to say. (Matt. 10:19-20)
- By reminding you what Jesus taught. (John 14:26)
- By enabling you to pray for others. (Rom. 8:26)
- By strengthening you. (Eph. 3:16)
- By developing hope in you through your trials. (Rom. 5:3-5)
- By giving you spiritual competence to minister. (2 Cor. 3:6)
- By producing in you the fruit of spiritual living. (Gal. 5:22-23)

Study these promises from God and depend on them. The Spirit is your guarantee that these promises are trustworthy.

Wayne Oates, in *The Christian Pastor*, identifies five ways in which the pastor undertakes the role of the Spirit in interpersonal relationships: (1) as *understanding friend*, (2) as *comforting strength*, (3) as *teacher*, (4) as *spiritual confidant*, and (5) as *healer*.[1] The purpose of this chapter is to explore the intertwined roles of the pastoral caregiver and the Holy Spirit in the practical ministry of hospital visitation.

Understanding Friend

This is the most basic level of pastoral care. You can be helpful to another person in hospital visitation only if you are known as a caring person, if you are trustworthy in your motives, and if you make yourself physically and emotionally available to others. Wayne Oates suggests that there are three characteristics of a helpful pastor: accurate empathy, nonpossessive warmth, and inherent genuineness.[2]

You are a person of understanding who is promised the help of the Holy Spirit in ministry. You possess the spiritual power of discernment (Phil. 1:9). The conversations that you have with others, though perhaps trivial on the surface, may possess deeper meaning than is obvious to others. The writer of Proverbs 20:5 says it most clearly: "The purposes of a man's heart are deep waters, but a man of understanding draws them out" (NIV). Discipline yourself to observe the significance of what you are experiencing. For instance, in the example that began this chapter, did you notice that the family groups are seated in different areas of the waiting room, separated by more than one or two seats? Did you observe the withdrawn, rigid postures and facial expressions of the families? Are your conversations with the families stilted in tone? You might expect to experience all of these situations if you know the family's history before you visit. If you do not know the family's history, ask a trusted colleague or lay leader in the church to help you. Remember, patient confidentiality is extremely important in this instance!

The key to being an understanding friend is *accurate empathy*. There is an old Irish story about two friends who are thoroughly inebriated, and even though they make elaborate promises about the depth of their friendship, one fellow begins to weep and accuse the other of insensitivity: "If you don't know what hurts me, how can you say that you love me?" Empathy alone is not enough. Our empathy must be focused accurately and felt deeply in order to help the spouses and families of the ill.

A word of caution: Never, ever, say "I know how you (must) feel," if you yourself have never been in the same situation. You cannot presume to know how another feels without asking, and you will forfeit any opportunity to be heard if you make unwarranted claims for yourself. Neither should you regale the patient, the spouse, or the family with similar tales from your own life. Focus your attention on them, and they will sense that you accurately understand their situation and care for them.

You are likely to hear the most heartbreaking, horrifying, and heartwarming stories in your hospital visitation. A *nonpossessive warmth* is an essential skill for developing an effective pastoral care ministry. Your role as an empathetic listener requires that you learn to "bracket" or "suspend" your own values and judgments as you listen to others. Listen to understand what is being said, and why, instead of listening to pass judgment. Follow the example of Jesus with the woman caught in adultery, and model love and compassion for the person rather than horror or outrage at the sin.

Some pastors feel the heightened presence of their own emotional needs when counseling others in the hospital. A crucial aspect of nonpossessive warmth is the ability to suspend your own needs in such a situation. Fred McGehee, who counseled many pastors in his work at the Southern Baptist Sunday School Board, described nonpossessive warmth as "being able to respond with affection to the other person's need rather than using the other person to meet one's own need."

A listening technique that may help you to practice nonpossessive warmth is "fogging." "Fogging" is described in *Listening and Caring Skills*, written by John Savage, as "naming the truth in another person's critical statements."[3] Savage suggests that "fogging" can take at least three forms:

1. You can agree with any statement that is true for you.
2. You can agree with any statement that may contain some truth.
3. You can agree with any statement that is a generalization, as long as it has some possibility of being true for you.

I used this technique when I served as a volunteer chaplain at a large metropolitan Atlanta hospital. Several times during my service there I was called to the emergency room late on Friday night or early Saturday morning to minister to a family who had suffered a tragedy. Frequently these calls were the result of automobile accidents that occurred while the driver was under the influence of drugs or alcohol. Family members, often still impaired themselves by drug or alcohol use, would call out to curse God for allowing such a terrible thing to happen to their loved one. They sometimes turned to me to confirm that life is cruel. My desire was to minister to grieving persons, not to correct their theology, but at the same time some of their accusations against God went beyond irony into blasphemy. On such occasions, my best response was to use "fogging": "You're right that life can be terribly unfair." "I understand why you are terribly upset" is another response that conveys compassion while maintaining integrity.

In being an understanding friend, you may be called on to interact with family members who have difficulty expressing their emotions in acceptable ways. Sometimes persons under stress will act out their anger, fear, or anxiety by becoming aggressive toward other family members, toward you, or possibly even toward the medical staff or physicians. You will justifiably earn the respect of others if you are able to speak caringly, calmly, and reasonably to help an out-of-control individual regain his composure.

On one occasion I had to intervene to separate a family member from a physician after a child died from meningitis despite heroic efforts by the medical team. A male family member sought out the physician as a target for his own rage, and was berating the physician mercilessly. I could tell that the physician, who himself was visibly distraught at the death of the child, was approaching the point where he would no longer tolerate the abuse. I walked over and softly suggested to the family member that the child's mother needed him to console her, and led him to another room to be with the grieving parents. During the walk to the other room, he composed himself, and there were no other outbursts from the family. The physician, who walked back to his office after his assailant left, later thanked me for handling the situation. Although this is a highly unusual circumstance, you may be called upon to handle such high-tension situations.

"Miss Mary" was a good-hearted simple country soul whose life revolved around caring for her husband, who was in the hospital again for the treatment of his decaying legs and feet. Miss Mary believed in feeding her husband all the foods he liked best, although the doctors told her that sweet foods were bad for his diabetes. The cycle of too much sugar and poor circulation had necessitated the doctor's decision to remove her husband's legs just below the hips. Miss Mary called her pastor and me to pray for her on the day before the surgery. We visited with her, and after our prayer together she began sobbing uncontrollably. After she had cried for several minutes, she caught her breath and looked at her pastor and me. Gesturing to a height of about three feet off the floor, she said, "But he's only going to be this tall." Only after we had exited the hospital completely did we turn to look at each other, and then we collapsed in hysterics. The situation was certainly not funny, but Miss Mary's explanation of it surely was!

Inherent genuineness, the third characteristic of a helpful pastor, suggests that the pastor who is comfortable in his own personhood will be able to be helpful to others. I will explore this truth further in the last chapter of this book.

Comforting Strength

The hymn of praise that begins 2 Corinthians sounds the downbeat for us in understanding how the pastor provides comforting strength for his flock through the presence of the Holy Spirit: "All praise to the God and Father of our Lord Jesus Christ. He is the source of every mercy and the God who comforts us. He comforts us in all our troubles so that we can comfort others. When others are troubled, we will be able to give them the same comfort God has given us. You can be sure that the more we suffer for Christ, the more God will shower us with his comfort through Christ" (2 Cor. 1:3-5 NLT). How comforting these words are to the pastoral caregiver, for they remind him that the strength he has to give to others comes from God, not solely from the strength of the pastor's own life.

Though they may not admit it, and indeed may seek to hide it from their loved one and you, the spouse and family of the patient are experiencing serious emotional distress. They sense from the patient any anxieties that he may have regarding death or the future. The family, especially the spouse, also experience isolation from the routines of life, from each other, and from friends. They need the comfort and strength of a pastor whose life is grounded in the empowering strength of the Holy Spirit.

Each spouse and each family is, of course, different, so you will have to rely on your own sense of how you are needed in each situation. It is permissible, though not often effective, to ask what you can do to be of help, for many parishioners will not want to burden you with their own "silly" needs. To give you a place to start, here are a few suggestions for ministering to the spouse and/or family: (1) Invite the family to share with you some of their family stories, (2) ask the spouse how they met their mate, (3) invite the spouse to go to lunch or to get coffee with you, (4) ask if they need their yard mowed during the hospital stay, (5) recommend a good book on a subject of interest and bring it with you on your next visit, (6) lend the family a "book on cassette" and a player (with earphones) for their use, (7) lend the family a copy of the New Testament on tape, (8) share with the spouse a favorite recording of music, (9) bring them a hometown newspaper, (10) offer to read to the patient, spouse, and family from the Scripture, or (11) if invited to do so, sit and "visit" with the family for a while. There are many possibilities, so let your imagination be your guide!

The birth of a child is an especially important opportunity to be a comforting strength to your parishioners. Few experiences in life can bring as much joy, or as much sorrow, as the birth of a child. Before you visit the new family, it is wise to check with the hospital concerning the specific visiting hours on the obstetric floor. When you arrive at the room, be especially careful in entering so that you do not embarrass yourself or the new mother. If in doubt, ask the nurse to check with the family for you. Make your visit brief and celebrative. Assure the new parents that they will not be alone in the process of raising their child and that their congregation cares for them. Praise God for the gift of the new child, and pray for the future health and security of the child. Be sure that you know the child's full name and birth statistics—the members of the congregation will want to know!

Don't forget that even the most anticipated and celebrated birth brings with it radical changes and deep anxieties. The routines of life, particularly for first-time parents, are about to change totally. The relationship of wife and husband will change with the addition of the child and will need to take on a greater maturity. Every new parent wonders, "Will I be a good parent?" The economic, time, energy, and emotional challenges of parenthood, which were previously theoretical, now seem intensely practical and provoke anxiety for the parents. In all of the excitement over the event and attention paid to the new arrival and to the new mom, don't neglect the new father. It is true that he is not as directly involved in the birth, but he may feel guilt over the pain his wife has experienced in childbirth, he may feel bewildered by his new responsibilities, and he may feel pushed aside by the newcomer in his house. He needs reassurance, too.

A birth to a single mother is a special event, as well. She will need the same celebration, sense of community, and reassurance that all new parents need as she faces the additional burden of raising a child by herself. An involved and caring pastor and congregation can give a single mother the hope that her child will have a safe and secure future. Take care to make sure she knows that she is welcome to participate in all of the rituals of your church for celebrating a birth.

Ministering to families whose child is stillborn or born with serious birth defects is a particularly difficult and important ministry. The need for the comforting strength of the minister may be particularly acute at the time of the birth. In either of these two situations, a wise pastor will want to pray with the family and for the child. Ask for, and use, the child's name in your prayers. If your religious tradition does not include a prayer book with suggested prayers for this situation, consider using some of the prayers that are included in the appendix to this book.

In the sad event of an infant death, be aware that the mother and father will want to hold and talk to their child. This is natural and an essential part of the grieving process. Reassure the parents of God's love for their child. The parents may want to know if their child will go to heaven. Answer affirmatively, and remind the parents of the story of Jesus blessing the children. This image will certainly provide comfort to them.

The birth of a child with serious birth defects is especially difficult because the child will be taken immediately to the neonatal intensive care unit. The parents likely will not have the same opportunities as other parents to hold their child and talk to her, and they may feel this lack of contact acutely. Plan to be present at the hospital more frequently than usual and stay in close contact with the family. The day will come when you will be allowed to make a pastoral visit to the baby, but you will probably make it in a disposable gown, mask, and perhaps even gloves. Make this visit as soon as you are allowed to do so. Your concern is a powerful comfort to the parents.

The anxiety level of the parents of children born with birth defects, or with Downs syndrome, is understandably high. In addition to the usual anxieties, these parents have special needs and worries. Your presence and prayers are your gift to these parents. Again, it is important to use the child's name as often and as naturally as possible. Celebrate this child as a special child. Concentrate on the events of each day, and share with the parents and family the value of faithful trust in God's provision.

Caring for a dying person and his family is another situation you will commonly face. The Gospel writers provide us with descriptions of how Jesus dealt with the family of a dying person in the story of Jairus's daughter (Matt. 9:18-26; Mark 5:21-43; Luke 8:40-56) and the story of the raising of Lazarus (John 11:1-44). From the accounts of these occurrences, we can identify six actions Jesus took in caring for the family of a dying person:

1. Jesus sought out the family of the dying because he had compassion on them.
2. Jesus focused his ministry on the immediate family (Mark).
3. His compassion did not depend on the faith of the individual family members, but came from his own character (Jairus's wife, Martha and Mary).
4. His healing included the family members, for example when Jesus told Jairus and his wife to go feed their daughter, as if to include them in the miracle and to convince them of their daughter's healing (Mark).
5. He led the family members to talk to each other (Mary and Martha).
6. Jesus offered to the family the hope and comfort of his resurrection (John).

What can you learn about ministry to the family from such a Bible study? Your own insights are your best guide, but here are five principles for ministry to the family of the dying: (1) Communicate often with the family, taking your clues for conversation from them; (2) facilitate conversation between the patient and each family member as well as between the family members; (3) never promise more than you can deliver, especially in praying for healing; (4) make the resurrection power of Jesus your bedrock conviction;

and (5) offer to the family the hope of healing or the hope of resurrection.

You may find that the direction of the conversation with the family or spouse disturbs you, particularly if you have difficulty talking about death. The spouse or family may talk about the patient in the past tense. They may share memories of happier days, choosing to remember their loved one as she was. They may ask painful questions, such as "What will we do without her?" They may even demand that you command God to heal their loved one, and then become angry if you cannot or will not do so. In their anger at their loved one for dying, or at God for allowing her to die, you—the representative of God—may become the target of their rage. They may speak rudely or angrily to you in acting out their own grief. Do not take this personally, but forgive them and accept them as Christ accepted the accusations and grief of Martha and Mary.

Caring for the spouse or family is acutely important in those experiences that might be described as *"worse than death"* experiences. What can be worse than having a loved one die? Some families find that permanently debilitating conditions, especially in cases of senility and dementia, such as Alzheimer's disease, are more stressful than dealing with the death of the loved one. Mental illnesses, particularly those that issue in violence or end in institutionalization, are a special kind of "hell on earth" for families. Caring for a comatose loved one, especially in cases where there is little or no hope of recovery and where the prognosis is for a life expectancy of many years, can destroy the strongest marriage or family.

What can you do for families in such pain? The most important thing is the simplest: Stay in touch with them and do not allow them to feel forgotten. Also, organize the church to provide relief for the caregivers and perhaps even a place for the family to go to "get away" for a while. The family may have exhausted its financial resources, and the opportunity to get away to a mountain cabin or a beach house may be greatly appreciated. Assure the family of your concern and demonstrate the constant commitment of the congregation to pray for the family. While these actions will not change the circumstances, they most certainly will convey the care of the Holy Spirit to the family. There is nothing that can comfort believers in this sort of situation like the promise of Scripture:

> Not only so, but we also rejoice in our sufferings, because we know that suffering produces perseverance; perseverance, character; and character, hope. And hope does not disappoint us, because God has poured out his love into our hearts by the Holy Spirit, whom he has given us. (Rom. 5:3-5 NIV)

Teacher

The intensity of the hospital experience can create a feeling of dislocation for the spouse and family of a patient. Their lives outside the hospital are temporarily put aside, and their attentions are focused on the care and condition of the loved one. This focus can disrupt their normal view of life, and into this disparity of worlds comes their pastor, whose opportunity it is to offer a whole and holy perspective of life. In this setting, the pastor's role is intertwined again with the work of the Holy Spirit in the lives of his parishioners: "But the Counselor, the Holy Spirit, whom the Father will send in my name, will teach you all things and will remind you of everything I have said to you" (John 14:26 NIV).

From a practical standpoint, the pastor can help the family learn to accept and acquiesce to the rules of hospital life. The following "rules" are distilled from twenty-five years of hospital visitation:

- The single most important aspect of hospital life to the hospital is accurate paperwork.
- Families are expected to do patient care.
- The hospital staff cannot operate on your timetable.
- Wash your hands often.
- Medical personnel are people, too.

These "rules" can be frustrating when a spouse or family is new to the hospital experience. The bureaucracy of the hospital, which can seem impersonal to the point of crassness, developed as a survival tool in our "lawsuit-mad" society. It is, therefore, all the more important to be sure that families have their legal affairs in order before they have need of them. There is no valid reason for any adult person to avoid drawing up a legal will, a living will, and a power-of-attorney document for use should the person become incapacitated. With the assistance of a helpful attorney, every church can offer to its congregants a seminar on the type and nature of the essential documents.

The other "rules" follow from the reality that most hospitals today are short on staffing, either due to a lack of available personnel or personnel costs. When fear for a loved one's health and exhaustion from long days and longer nights collides with a medical staff with too many tasks and not enough hands, the result can be harmful for all concerned. A caring pastor can offer the family a kind word of instruction that may defuse an emotionally traumatic situation.

The caring, consistent presence of a pastoral caregiver can also teach a hurting family how to live with patience in the uncertainty of illness. So often, the family has internalized the medical drama portrayed by the medical shows on the television, in which the illness and treatment of disease are compressed into the requirements of a one-hour television show. Reality makes a lie of this neatly packaged view of illness. Much of the time, the only hope for the cure of a patient is the tincture of time, and despite the best education, experience, and tools of modern medicine, patience is the most helpful characteristic that a spouse or family can possess.

Another gift that a sensitive pastor can give a spouse is the awareness that he or she is under an enormous amount of stress. Many spouses attempt to deflect any attempt to ask them to care for themselves, usually for the reason that they only want to be with their loved one. The reality is, however, that a person under a great deal of emotional stress is unable to be "present" for others. The burden of caring for another can break the caregiver's physical or emotional health. By suggesting that the spouse should care for himself or herself, the pastor may help a loving family care for a hurting spouse.

Perhaps the greatest opportunity that the pastor has for teaching her hospital-bound parishioners is in answering the questions of a religious nature that arise naturally in the course of hospitalization. These frequently involve the issues of salvation, suffering and the Christian faith, and heaven. "Will I ever see my loved one again?" is a question that every pastor will hear, as well as "Will I know my loved one when I get to heaven?" The more basic question of "Who gets to go to heaven?" is also common, and sometimes personalized: "Will my loved one go to heaven?" You will answer these questions as straightforwardly as you can, but remember that the primary need behind the question may be for reassurance rather than for education. It is wise to come to an understanding yourself of these issues in the context of your own faith tradition. An older pastor may be your best source of help.

Spiritual Confidant

The confession of sins plays an important role in the Christian faith, whether that confession is made to a priest, a pastor, another Christian, or directly to God. No matter how formal or informal the pattern of confession in your faith tradition, you will find yourself hearing bedside confessions in your hospital ministry. It is an instinctive drive in persons with religious convictions to free themselves of the power of unconfessed sin before facing death or even surgery. The forms that these confessions take may vary dramatically, but the perceived need for them is intense. If the patient comes from a faith tradition where confession is not formalized, the confession might sound as if the patient is telling a story about an event in the past without a direct request for absolution or forgiveness. In other cases, the confession may be gut-wrenchingly personal. Whatever the nature of the confession, you, as the representative of God, are being asked for the reassurance that prayers for forgiveness are heard and answered by God. I have found that the most meaningful response to confession is to invite the person to confess his sins to God in prayer, and then to pray to God that the confessor might know the joy of divine forgiveness. There are prayers for forgiveness included in the appendix to this book if your denomination does not already suggest prayers for you to use.

What if the "confession" sounds to you to be more of a rationalization or justification of the person's actions, rather than an actual confession? Certainly a brief teaching on the nature of contrition (use a shorter and simpler word) is warranted, but what to do next? Let your specific denominational training and personal theology be your guide. Perhaps this is an opportunity to practice the "nonpossessive warmth" described earlier.

In the case study presented at the first of this chapter, Mr. Riley is actually making the beginning of a personal confession by repeating "I've lived a good life." It sounds as though he may have regrets that burden him. Perhaps an effective response might be: "Are there parts of your life you would like to talk about that are not good?" Assuming you have the privacy that you need and the patient is willing, you are now able to help the patient put part of his past behind him. The spouse or family of the patient may very well need to talk to you in your role as pastoral confessor.

Healer

In the Gospels, whenever Jesus encounters a family member alongside an ill person, he always seems to include the family in the healing. From the story of Jairus's daughter to the story of the man born blind to the story of Jesus casting demons into pigs, the healing ministry of Jesus included compassion for the family of the ill person. In your hospital visitation, you, too, will encounter patients, spouses, and families that need God's healing touch.

There is a movement abroad in all denominations for the ill person to request prayer and the ministry of healing from the pastors and elders of the church. This ministry is definitely biblical, but is foreign to many faith traditions that pride themselves on biblical literalism. How will you deal with this issue, especially if it arises in the context of hospital visitation? My suggestion would be that you take the request literally and grant it if you can. The healing, if it comes, will be from God and not from you; nor will the healing depend solely on your faith. So read the Scriptures, arm yourself with the Spirit of Christ, and act in faith in the God who called you to this ministry.

More often than a ministry of healing, however, you will be called to a ministry of healing emotions and spiritual confusion. The greatest enemy of most Christians is their own ignorance of the loving, forgiving, healing nature of God. You will be asked in other terms, but your most common calling will be to heal a person's inadequate understanding of God as loving or of herself as loved by God. In the face of all the trials of hospital visitation, this is one of its greatest joys—to share the unconditional love and care of God with a seeking person.

Sometimes you will have the unpleasant duty of attempting to help a feuding family disarm and reconcile. The stresses produced by the illness of a parent can cause a previously tranquil family to expose its dysfunctionalities to public view. In the words of Wayne Oates: "The politics of the inner circle of family conflict are *power politics*. Who is going to control whom, and who has to knuckle under to whom? This struggle with the clans and between clans regularly traces back to arguments over the birthright, to occasions when trickery took place."[4]

A family experiences crisis when the strategies that it previously used for resolving conflict prove inadequate to its present challenges. A sensitive pastor can assess whether this seems to be the case, and can suggest new coping skills to help the family survive the crisis period. One way a pastor can do this is by suggesting that the family fall back on a (previous) image of itself as loving and supportive of the patient. His prayers for the family, as well as his steadfast refusal to take sides in the argument, may give the family the resources they need to function for the moment and to enable them to provide needed support to the patient. It may also be wise for the pastor to suggest that the family see a qualified therapist for counseling after the crisis period has passed for the patient.[5]

In this chapter, I have suggested that the work of the pastoral caregiver is intertwined with the work of the Holy Spirit, and that resources available to the pastor through the power of the Holy Spirit are adequate spiritually for every situation that she will face. Take this promise as your own: "He has made us competent as ministers of a new covenant—not of the letter but of the Spirit; for the letter kills, but the Spirit gives life" (2 Cor. 3:6 NIV).

Notes

1. Wayne E. Oates, *The Christian Pastor,* third edition (Philadelphia: Westminster Press, 1982), pp. 86-87.

2. Ibid., p. 79.

3. John Savage, *Listening and Caring Skills in Ministry: A Guide for Pastors, Counselors, and Small Groups* (Nashville: Abingdon Press, 1996), pp. 57-61.

4. Wayne E. Oates, *The Presence of God in Pastoral Counseling* (Waco, Tex.: Word, 1986), p. 58.

5. Edward P. Wimberly, *African American Pastoral Care* (Nashville: Abingdon Press, 1991), pp. 74-75.

CHAPTER FOUR

The Pastor as Shepherd: Relating to the Congregation

Mr. Dixon, a generous, beloved business owner and deacon in the church, enters the hospital for tests, assuming that his tireless efforts to better his community and to serve his church have simply exhausted him, and that he will need to learn to take better care of himself. The report from the physician is far more terrifying, however. Mr. Dixon learns that he suffers from ALS, also known as Lou Gehrig's disease, and that he faces the progressive loss of his motor skills and a lingering death. Mr. Dixon, his wife, children, and his extended family are devastated by this diagnosis, of course, but the impact on the community is also profound. From the children on the sports teams that his business sponsors, to the clients who utilize his business services, to the senior adults in the community who benefit from his generosity and visits, to the friends in his church family, the news of Mr. Dixon's illness hangs over the community like the sound of a siren in the air on the first night that your teenager drives to a friend's house on her own. You feel that everyone in your town is looking to you for help in their distress, whether or not they are "members" of your flock.

Shepherding the Flock

The biblical image of the pastor as "shepherd" is the primary image of that role in the New Testament. Jesus identified himself as a shepherd, and you are a shepherd, too. How can the same image that applied to our Savior apply to a busy twenty-first-century pastor like you? Review the tasks of the shepherd for a moment:

- to lead the flock (Ps. 77:20)
- to protect the flock (1 Sam. 17:34-36; John 10:1)
- to provide rest for the flock (Ps. 23:2)
- to find water for the flock (Gen. 29:2-10)
- to care for the sick sheep of the flock (Ezek. 34:16)
- to know each member of the flock by name (John 10:3-5)
- to count the flock (Jer. 33:13)
- to search for the lost sheep of the flock (Luke 15:4-5)

Take the time to read each of these scriptures, then ask yourself: *Isn't this what God called me to do?* If being a shepherd was good enough for Abraham, Jacob, Moses, David, Jesus, and Rachel, isn't it a proper description of your pastoral ministry?

A word of warning—God promises a severe judgment for shepherds who ignore their responsibilities. The judgment found in Ezekiel 34:7-10 applies to shepherds of all times and places:

> Therefore, you shepherds, hear the word of the LORD: As surely as I live, says the Sovereign LORD, you abandoned my flock and left them to be attacked by every wild animal. Though you were my shepherds, you didn't search for my sheep when they were lost. You took care of yourselves and left the sheep to starve. Therefore, you shepherds, hear the word of the LORD. This is what the Sovereign LORD says: I now consider

these shepherds my enemies, and I will hold them responsible for what has happened to my flock. I will take away their right to feed the flock, along with their right to feed themselves. I will rescue my flock from their mouths; the sheep will no longer be their prey. (NLT)

Shepherding the flock means building a relationship with the individuals who are in your flock. The kind of relationship that you have with your congregation depends on your personality and ministry style as you encounter the spoken and unspoken expectations of your flock. The essential emotional tie between you and your congregation must be trust that you will shepherd them to the best of your abilities. In a massive survey of twelve thousand persons, both lay and clergy, from forty-seven denominations, Daniel Aleshire described the most expected characteristic of a pastor as that of "handling stressful situations by remaining calm under pressure while continuing to affirm persons."[1] Just reading that statement makes you nervous, doesn't it? How will you develop the grace, poise, and courage to earn such a reputation?

The source of the pastor's strength and his motivation for service is described powerfully by Eugene Peterson in his paraphrase of 1 Peter 5:1-6:

I have a special concern for you church leaders. I know what it's like to be a leader, in on Christ's sufferings as well as the coming glory. Here's my concern: that you care for God's flock with all the diligence of a shepherd. Not because you have to, but because you want to please God. Not calculating what you can get out of it, but acting spontaneously. Not bossily telling others what to do, but tenderly showing them the way.

When God, who is the best shepherd of all, comes out in the open with his rule, he'll see that you've done it right and commend you lavishly. And you who are younger must follow your leaders. But all of you, leaders and followers alike, are to be down to earth with each other, for—

> "God has had it with the proud,
> But takes delight in just plain people."

So be content with who you are, and don't put on airs. God's strong hand is on you; he'll promote you at the right time. Live carefree before God; he is most careful with you. (*The Message*)

What a powerful promise! You can shepherd your flock in spontaneous joy and obedience to God, living in the faith that his care for you is all of the strength, wisdom, and motivation you will ever need.

Shepherding the flock means guiding the flock. Like sheep, the persons in our care depend on us to lead them to the resources that will sustain them and nourish them in their lives and in their illnesses. Where will you lead them? I am convinced that the role of the pastor is to provide spiritual care for his congregation, and therefore his role is to lead them to spiritual resources. The compassionate shepherd regards hospital visitation as an opportunity to guide the flock into a deeper experience of prayer, to teach the flock about the depth of God's care for them, and to interpret the meaning of illness and tragedy in a way that does justice to both the patient and to God.

Robert Coles, in an essay on pastoral care, pointed out that members of the clergy sometimes forget their role as spiritual guide. He recounts the story of a sick friend who was visited by a priest. The friend responded to the priest's opening question by stating that he felt "fine," by which he meant that he had no desire to answer further questions in that direction. The priest, who misunderstood the answer to convey a reticence to open up emotionally, proceeded to probe at great length into the patient's emotional state. After the priest left, the patient became outraged at the lack of spiritual care that he received. In Coles's words:

> He had wanted to talk with the priest about God and His ways, about Christ's life and death . . . about Heaven and Hell—only to be approached repeatedly with psychological words and phrases. In their entirety those words and phrases constituted a statement, an insinuation: you are in psychological jeopardy, and that is what I, an ordained priest of the Holy Roman Catholic Church, have learned to consider more important than anything else, when in the presence of a person such as you.[2]

I have observed the same behavior in clergy of other denominations and even, God forbid, in myself.

How can we minister more caringly and effectively than by teaching our flock how to pray, especially in their illnesses and in the face of death? There is no lack of resources, so choose one, study it thoroughly yourself, and teach it to your people. They will count themselves fortunate to have such a wise and caring pastor.

Another function of the shepherd is her role as a teacher. Your ministry in teaching the patient is covered earlier in this book, but an illness like that of Mr. Dixon is also an opportunity to teach the congregation vicariously about matters of life and death. Many congregations have midweek prayer services, and these can be powerful times for teaching. Most of the time these services become opportunities for praying for others, and sometimes degenerate into what my seminary friends called "hangnail" prayers, as in "Please pray for my aunt Mary. She has a hangnail." In the case of Mr. Dixon, there is no cure for his condition short of divine intervention, and this presents an occasion for teaching the congregation that prayer is sometimes a long-term process or even that "precious in the eyes of the Lord is the death of his saints." Making progress reports weekly to those attending the prayer meeting assures the congregation that you are visiting the hospitals regularly, and that you will keep them informed appropriately.

Shepherding the flock means keeping confidences. In your hospital visitation, people will behave in a variety of ways, from "keeping a stiff upper lip" and maintaining an emotionally reserved posture to going "over the top" in their behavior and acting out their frustration, rage, and pain in inappropriate and even self-destructive ways. However you encounter them, those you visit have the right to expect you to treat their words and actions with discretion and in confidence. You will learn to visit patients and their family and keep their confidences, or you will pay a high price for your indiscretion. Outside of your spiritual role as pastoral caregiver, you have no higher responsibility than that of maintaining patient confidentiality.

Fortunately, there are some simple tools you can use in communicating the condition of the patient to those who care about her without violating her confidence. The first is to ask the patient and the family: "What would you like me to tell others about how you are doing?" By asking the patient's or family's guidance, you have demonstrated respect for them and discovered the content of what you may report to others in good faith. Another acceptable tool is to ask the patient: "Do you mind if I share this report with the congregation?" or "Would it be okay if I told others what you just said?" You can modify your question to suit your relationship with the patient while gaining permission to tell the patient's story to others.

On occasion you may have the experience of hearing something from the patient that he does not wish for you to share with his family. This places you in a sensitive position, because most families assume that you will share your conversations and your impressions of the patient with them, and usually you can without violating a confidence. In this instance, it is wise to state kindly but firmly: "I am sorry, but the conversations that I have with people are confidential. I do not have permission to tell you more than I already have." While you may encounter anger from some people, you will also gain the respect of the majority by reassuring them that what they say to you will be held in confidence.

In our present legal environment of proliferating lawsuits, most hospitals are extremely careful to observe strict rules regarding issues of confidentiality, and they hold their medical and administrative employees to a high standard of accountability on this issue. While you are not an employee of a hospital, if you violate the principles of confidentiality, you may find that you are unwelcome in a specific hospital. You will, at a minimum, lose the respect and help of persons who are treating the members of your congregation. If in doubt, don't say it!

Shepherding the flock sometimes means standing as an advocate for them before God. Like the prophets of the Old Testament, you may want and need to stand before God and ask, "How long, O Lord will you be silent?" Mr. Dixon and his family suffered silently, believing that their faith strengthened them to bear the burdens they faced without complaint. Others, however, may need the catharsis of confronting God about the unfairness of their plight. For myself, I have stood before God in anger and bewilderment at the suffering and the incomprehensible perversity of life. There is, of course, a risk in saying to the congregation that you cannot understand why Mr. Dixon and his family suffer so much and so long, and that you find yourself at a loss to understand why, and this makes you angry. It is much safer to stay with time-tested and honorable statements of faith. Only you can decide how transparent you can afford to be before your flock, but know that at least some of the flock would rather trust a shepherd who knows their pain and will confront it honestly.

Shepherding the flock means doing the little things well. Here are some practical reminders for being an effective hospital visitor:

- Always take business cards into the hospital with you. You may need to leave a note if the patient is asleep, in another part of the hospital for tests, or otherwise unavailable.

- Some pastoral caregivers leave prayer cards with the patient or family. Printed on the card is an appropriate prayer and/or Scripture selection, along with the pastor's name and the church phone number. These also can be used in the place of business cards to indicate that the pastor has visited and was unable to speak with the patient.

- Work the "edges" of your church congregation. Those near the center of the church's activity will be well cared for by other members of the flock. Those at the edges will be less so. "The artful shepherd," said Phillips Brooks, will track the edges like a sheep dog, herding the strays in towards the center.[3]

- Whatever the level of education you have earned or will earn, it is wise to avoid using the honorific title "Doctor" in a hospital. As a friend of mine found out, you can be embarrassed quickly if you do. He knocked, called out his name, and entered the hospital room of a relative of one of the members of his congregation. The patient, a female, did not know the pastor, and was suffering some pain from a pelvic incision, so when he stood by her bed, she pulled back the bedclothes to show him where it hurt! She was embarrassed, he was embarrassed, and the relative was mortified with the outcome of his visit. A little humility prevents a lot of humiliation. Besides the possibility of suffering embarrassment, I have found that I receive more respect and cooperation from physicians when I use the term "Reverend" or its equal, even when the doctor knows of my title.

Shepherding a Community

You are a marked person, especially if you pastor a church in a small community. You will be called by your role—"preacher," "padre," "rev," "brother," "sister," or "pastor"—even by persons who would never think of darkening the door of your church. You will be watched carefully and judged by how you do even the smallest things. No part of your life is too insignificant for notice by the community. If you prove to be a trustworthy person, and a person of integrity, you will be approached by people in the community to visit a loved one in the hospital. "Preacher, if you're over at the hospital anyway, would you mind checking in on my (fill in the blank here). Don't go to any trouble, now." This is as high a compliment as many people will ever be able to pay you. You are trusted to care, and your ministry is sought by persons who may scoff at the idea of having a Christian faith for themselves. If asked, and if you agree, go! This is an opportunity for genuine evangelism, and a cry for help.

Also, if you shepherd a small congregation or pastor in a small town, you may be able to share pastoral duties with a trusted pastor friend when you need to be away from the congregation. In that situation, most congregations will gladly accept the ministry of a neighboring pastor. I have visited congregants in a number of different denominations and have always been warmly received when I explained that the patient's pastor is away and that I am "on call" for her or for him. This is a common occurrence for physicians, why not for pastors?

The Pastor as Healer

While most Christians believe that the healing of the body is described in the New Testament and that it is commended for the church, there is no consensus on how this is to be achieved today. That Jesus healed the sick and lame is clear; there are fourteen distinct instances of physical or mental healing described in the Gospels. Jesus commissioned his disciples to carry out this ministry of healing even without his physical presence:

> When Jesus had called the Twelve together, he gave them power and authority to drive out all demons and to cure diseases, and he sent them out to preach the kingdom of God and to heal the sick. He told them: "Take nothing for the journey—no staff, no bag, no bread, no money, no extra tunic. Whatever house you enter, stay there until you leave that town. If people do not welcome you, shake the dust off your feet when you leave their town, as a testimony against them." So they set out and went from village to village, preaching the gospel and healing people everywhere. (Luke 9:1-6 NIV)

To this description, the Gospel of Mark adds the following: "They drove out many demons and anointed many sick people with oil and healed them" (Mark 6:13 NIV).

This ministry of healing extended beyond the earthly life of Jesus. As described in Acts 5:16 (NIV): "Crowds gathered also from the towns around Jerusalem, bringing their sick and those tormented by evil spirits, and all of them were healed." The spiritual gift of healing is listed in 1 Corinthians 12:9 (NIV): ". . . to another faith by the same Spirit, to another gifts of healing by that one Spirit." James 5:14-16 records another instance where healing is commended to the church:

> Is any one of you sick? He should call the elders of the church to pray over him and anoint him with oil in the name of the Lord. And the prayer offered in faith will make the sick person well; the Lord will raise him up. If he has sinned, he will be forgiven. Therefore confess your sins to each other and pray for each other so that you may be healed. The prayer of a righteous man is powerful and effective. (NIV)

It is clear that Jesus practiced physical healing, that he commissioned his disciples to continue this ministry, that the Holy Spirit gives the gift of healing to some people, and that the early church practiced healing as a form of worship. How does this apply to a twenty-first-century pastor doing hospital visitation? Simply, you may be expected to carry out this practice in your visiting. What if you do not claim the spiritual gift of healing as yours? You can still carry out the practices described in the passage in James. How will you plan a spiritual ministry of healing if the idea is strange or unfamiliar to you? Read the instructions in James, interpret them as best you can, teach your congregation what you are going to do, and, in prayer and dependence on the Holy Spirit, just do it. There may be a long tradition of healing services in your faith expression; if so, follow the forms prescribed. They have the advantage of experience on their side.

There is one additional example of Jesus' that we should follow in the practice of healing today. Jesus consistently warned those whom he healed not to tell others what had happened to them. While there are valid hermeneutical reasons to interpret this warning in other contexts, the simple meaning of the text still stands. Jesus sought to maintain the privacy of the healed, and he avoided turning healing into a sideshow. His example should be our practice.

Story Gathering and Storytelling

Biblical scholar Raymond E. Brown places the site of the annunciation of the birth of Jesus to the shepherds by the angels at Migdal-eder, "the tower of the flock," a watchtower for shepherds located on the road from Jerusalem to Bethlehem. In this way he connects the birth of Jesus with Bethlehem, citing Genesis 35:21 and Micah 4:8 as supporting this theory.[4] As shepherds were usually solitary characters, choosing to keep their flocks separate from one another, why would they have chosen to group themselves together? It is, of course, purely speculative, but my guess is that the shepherds took advantage of this watchtower to be together and to do what people of all vocations do whenever they have the opportunity to be together—they tell stories!

Edward P. Wimberly, in *African American Pastoral Care*, characterizes the importance of the role of narrative in pastoral care: "Genuine pastoral care from a narrative perspective involves the use of stories by pastors in ways that help persons and families to visualize how and where God is at work in their lives and thereby receive healing and wholeness."[5] Every prayer meeting, every intercessory prayer session with other Christians, and every inquiry by a concerned friend is a possible opportunity to tell a story. You, the shepherd, have a privileged perspective on this story, and the opportunity to help a hurting patient or family use their story to bring comfort or healing.

Words are for communication; stories bring communion. Eugene Peterson writes of taking his daughter, who was nine years old at the time, with him in making calls to nursing homes. Together they visited one elderly lady, who told them over and over again the same story about her childhood. After a time Peterson wearied of this visit, carried out his pastoral duties, and left. As he and his daughter rode along together, he commended her for her patience in listening to the lady's stories, and remarked that the lady's mind was not working like other people's. His daughter replied: "Oh, I knew that, Daddy; she was not trying to tell us anything, she was telling us who she is."[6]

Try listening to the stories that patients and families tell you about themselves. As you practice the skills of listening and interpreting, you will gain a valuable tool for ministry. John Savage suggests listening to stories on four levels:[7]

- Data back then
- Feelings back then
- Feelings now
- Self-disclosure (or the moment of "Aha!")

Use the listening skills described in an earlier chapter of this book, and soon you will be able to use stories as truth and as a place to begin the process of healing. But remember, each person's life is both a story and a process, and the end of the story cannot yet be told. You can bring perspective to the storyteller and the story, thus emulating the role of Jesus as shepherd and story-teller. Within the limits of confidentiality and with the permission of the teller, sprinkle your teaching and preaching with stories of faith and doubt, peace and conflict, and you will connect with your hearers at the level of the self.

C. S. Lewis wrote in *Christian Reflections*, "We ride with our backs to the engine. We have no notion what stage in the journey we have reached. . . . A story is precisely the sort of thing that cannot be understood till you have heard the whole of it."[8] As you listen to the stories that you will hear in the hospital, you can guide the storytellers to the "author and finisher of our faith," and the Master Storyteller, even Jesus our Lord.

Notes

1. Daniel O. Aleshire, "Eleven Major Areas of Ministry," in *Ministry in America* (New York: Harper & Row, 1980), p. 31.

2. Robert Coles, *Harvard Diary: Reflections on the Sacred and Secular* (New York: Crossroad), pp. 10-11.

3. Quoted in John Killinger, *The Tender Shepherd* (Nashville: Abingdon Press, 1985), p. 14.

4. Raymond E. Brown, *The Birth of the Messiah,* 2nd edition (New York: Doubleday, 1993), pp. 421-23.

5. Edward P. Wimberly, *African American Pastoral Care* (Nashville: Abingdon Press, 1991), p. 9.

6. Eugene Peterson, "Novelists, Pastors, and Poets," in *Subversive Spirituality,* ed. Jim Lyster et al. (Grand Rapids: Eerdmans, 1997), p. 178.

7. John Savage, *Listening and Caring Skills in Ministry: A Guide for Pastors, Counselors, and Small Groups* (Nashville: Abingdon Press, 1996), p. 79.

8. C. S. Lewis, *Christian Reflections* (Grand Rapids: Eerdmans, 1967), p. 106.

CHAPTER FIVE

The Pastor as Colleague: Relating to Other Caregivers

Suppose you are away at a denominational conference, and during your absence, Randy Dunn, a thirty-some-thing dad who is a member of your church, has a heart attack. His medical crisis is stabilized and, though he will undergo further medical tests, he is no longer in danger of dying. You are too far from the hospital to be present with the wife and family and to bring them the pastoral care they need. How will you handle this situation?

You have the following options:

- You can call another member of your ministerial staff to make this call for you.
- You may call another pastoral minister of your faith tradition who lives nearby and with whom you have a good relationship.
- You may call a pastor friend who lives in your community and possibly knows the patient.
- You may call a lay minister in your church whom you have trained to make pastoral calls. (You mean you haven't done this yet?)
- You may contact the volunteer chaplain on duty at the hospital to assess the situation.
- You may contact the staff hospital chaplain to seek her help in ministering to the family.

Each of these is a useful way of dealing with such a situation, and I have used each, but thrice blessed is the pastor who can share her ministry with a hospital chaplain who is well trained, sympathetic to the work of the pastor, and willing to partner with the pastor in the ministry of hospital visitation. Perhaps I have just been fortunate, but I have been blessed to minister alongside hospital chaplains who are among the most caring, dedicated, and professional caregivers I know.

How Does One Become a Chaplain?

Chaplains are extensively educated individuals. Generally, they are college and seminary graduates who extend their education by completing two units of Clinical Pastoral Education at an approved hospital. Included in the CPE training is intensive "hands-on" experience in each area of the hospital. Chaplain-trainees do a "rotation" in each of the major areas in a manner similar to the system used to train physicians. Chaplains come from diverse backgrounds: parish ministers, counselors, church staff ministers, and the military, just to list a few possibilities. They are usually ordained ministers in some faith tradition, and they are normally commissioned for the chaplaincy by the same denomination.

What is CPE? Clinical Pastoral Education was begun in 1925 as a form of theological education that takes place not exclusively in academic classrooms, but also in clinical settings where ministry is being practiced. CPE is offered in hospitals and healthcare institutions including private, university, military, and veterans' facilities; in prisons and correctional institutions; in parishes and congregations; in hospices and other places that care for the dying; in psychiatric facilities and community care; in business, industry, and other workplace settings; in retirement homes and geriatric centers; in rehabilitation centers such as those for physical illness and injury as well as those working with the addicted; and in communities, both urban and rural. The textbooks for CPE include in-depth study of "the living human documents." "Living human documents" means the people who receive care as well as the givers of care. Through the practice of ministry and the reflection thereon with supervisor and peers, the experiential learning that is CPE takes place.

The next step in becoming a hospital chaplain is obvious: Find an employer. Hospitals are not required by the Joint Committee on Accreditation of Hospitals (JCAHO), which sets the standards of practice for hospitals in the United States, to provide either a chaplain or a pastoral care department in a hospital. Many, if not most, larger and urban hospitals provide the care of chaplains for the patients, families, and staff. Most smaller and more rural hospitals have a staff of volunteer chaplains, most of whom have not had the opportunity to learn in a CPE program. I served as a volunteer chaplain in the Gwinnett Hospital System in metro Atlanta during the years in which it was establishing its professional chaplaincy department.

Why Does a Hospital Have Chaplaincy Staff?

The Mission Statement of the Pastoral Care Department of the Baptist Health Systems of South Florida* provides the most clear and concise rationale for having a pastoral care department (I will use the terms "chaplaincy" and "pastoral care department" inter-changeably) that I have read:

> Baptist Health Systems believes that a healthy connec-tion to God is vital to a person's physical, psychological and social well being. Research has demonstrated a clear relationship between spirituality and the process of

* Mission statement taken from the Web site of Baptist Health Systems of South Florida (http://www.baptisthealth.net) Used by permission.

healing. Our chaplains, representing a number of religious faiths, have received specialized training to provide emotional and spiritual support to patients and their families in times of need.

This statement does come from a healthcare system affiliated with a Christian denomination, and therefore the religious connection between faith and healing is explicit. But notice that even in this instance, the word *spirituality*, rather than the word *faith* is used. Many hospital administrators, lawyers, and physicians are reluctant to use religious language, even when the hospital is affiliated with a Christian denomination. In for-profit and government-sponsored hospitals, the connection between religious conviction and healing is generally less emphasized, and the importance of "caring for the patient" rather than "providing spiritual support" is primary. Whenever you enter a hospital facility, remember that you are not on your home turf and you should be sensitive to the hospital's standards for chaplains.

Hospital administrators are in a difficult position, and it is wise for the pastor to be sensitive to the dilemmas they face. Many if not most, hospital administrators wish to provide chaplains for the patients, but they must also confront these facts:

1. Medical personnel are required to maintain a rigorous schedule of continuing education, whereas pastors are not, so sometimes medical personnel regard pastors as under-trained and unprofessional.
2. Sometimes pastors, in their enthusiasm for serving God, are insensitive to the religious beliefs of patients of other faith traditions or of no religious faith at all.
3. Hospitals are not reimbursed by insurance companies for the care given by their chaplains. With

the rising costs of medical care and with declining levels of reimbursement due to managed care, hospital administrators bear the responsibility for trying to justify pastoral care departments from the standpoint of economic viability, and this is difficult to do.

In order to avoid the liabilities of untrained chaplains, however, hospitals establish departments of pastoral care to demonstrate a legally defensible standard of care. In the revisions of its standards for the year 2000, the Joint Commission on Accreditation of Healthcare Organizations (JCAHO)* even provides eight "examples of evidence of performance" that hospitals should meet in the area of pastoral care:

A. Recognition of the spiritual needs and rights of the person is reflected in policies, procedures, and administration's ability to articulate these needs and rights.
B. The Pastoral Services Department has a personnel ratio sufficient to meet and implement the goals and objectives of the department.
C. A formal arrangement is documented when the operational needs require pastoral personnel from outside the facility.
D. Members of the Pastoral Services staff are professionally trained and maintain or upgrade their skills consistent with other health care professionals.
E. Staff demonstrates ability to minister with persons of diverse cultural and religious backgrounds.
F. The Director is certified by a national professional chaplaincy organization and has a graduate theological degree and four units of CPE.

• Joint Commission CAMH 2001 Comprehensive Accreditation Manual for Hospitals, Examples of Implementation for RI 1 3 5. Oakbrook Terrace, Ill.: Joint Commission on Accreditation of Healthcare Organizations, copyright © 2001, pp. RI-29. Used by permission.

    G. Pastoral Services has identified comprehensive resources available for pastoral counseling, spiritual direction and other specific spiritual care services.

    H. The pastoral services staff document their interventions in the record of the patient.

As you can see, providing a chaplain has become a major investment of time and resources for the hospitals, and hospitals justifiably expect chaplains to meet the standards set for them. I have included this information in this chapter just so you realize what unknown (to pastors) expectations exist for your hospital chaplain.

A hospital chaplain once told me about an earnest and good-hearted minister who was trying to "lead a patient to Christ." That the patient happened to have been in a coma for a month was not a problem for this pastor. As he told the chaplain, "If he can hear me as you say he can, maybe he can get saved." The chaplain, himself a good-hearted individual, pointed out to the pastor that the patient would be unable to respond to his invitation, and besides, he was getting in the way of the intensive care medical staff. Such behavior horrifies most administrators, and in order to avoid it, they sometimes restrict the access of pastor to patient. Don't be guilty of making it more difficult for other pastors to minister to their own patients because of your insensitivity!

What Does a Chaplain Do?

A chaplain has a full-time job. A chaplain is usually available twenty-four hours a day, seven days a week, and 365 days a year in most larger hospitals, so there are long hours to fill. Chaplains make daily rounds, usually on their own, but sometimes with the medical staff. Some pastoral care departments assign chaplains to specific floors or to specific care areas of the hospital; others go where they are most needed at the time.

The Presbyterian Hospital of Albuquerque, New Mexico, provides on its Web site (www.phs.org/pastoralcare/pcstandards.htm) a specific and comprehensive listing of the standards of spiritual care for a chaplain:

1. Chaplains will serve all persons without prejudice; the spiritual traditions and practices of all persons will be respected and facilitated; and chaplains will not proselytize.
2. Pastoral care providers are either certified chaplains or under the direct supervision of certified, supervising chaplains.
3. Chaplains are active members of the interdisciplinary team—the totality of health includes body, mind, and spirit.
4. Clinical Pathway indicators guide other care team members in the effective use of chaplains.
5. Pastoral Care plays a key role in care of persons undergoing major life changes, or who are dying.
6. Chaplains assist patients, families, and staff, who are facing ethical or moral health care decisions, experiencing emotional difficulties around health concerns, or require or request crisis counseling.
7. Chaplains make a prompt and effective response to requests for pastoral care from patients, family members, and staff.
8. Chaplains make referral to and seek consultation with patients' spiritual resources in the community.
9. Chaplains assist with social and/or financial needs of patients/families not otherwise addressed by means of the "Chaplain's Fund" program.
10. Chaplains play an essential role in assisting with Advance Directives and the Organ Donor process.
11. Chaplains use spiritual, family, emotional, and

developmental histories to provide indicators for prevention program(s), health maintenance (wellness), and/or treatment intervention(s).

12. Chaplains provide information, education, and support to improve the total health of patients and plan members.

13. The Pastoral Care Department provides training in pastoral care for lay and ordained ministers.*

Like most pastors, however, the formal requirements of her job are just the starting place for the ministry of the hospital chaplain. As a caregiver, the chaplain is a relationship builder with patients, families, and staff. As a counselor, she is a midwife—guiding persons through the pain of transitions in health and relationships. As a member of the hospital staff, she is not there to practice medicine, but to use her skill in the spiritual art of healing. Her primary technique for healing is the judicious use of conversation and the practice of prayer. As the resident theologian, she does not explain the purpose of pain, suffering, or disease, but affirms that each person has worth in the eyes of the Creator, who is ultimately redemptive in purpose. Her credibility is built on trust, and trust requires that she never, ever, promise more from herself or her God than she can deliver.

Does this sound like an impossible job? Probably so to most people, but as a pastor you already know about the impossibility of fulfilling the expectations that others have for you. Like you, the chaplain is never "off duty" and is always "under the microscope" of the expectations of others. The chaplain knows what your job is like. Wouldn't you like to have this kind of friend and colleague?

---

* Presbyterian Hospital of Albuquerque, New Mexico, provides on its Web site (ww.phs.org/pastoralcare/pcstandards.htm) a specific and comprehensive listing of the standards of spiritual care for a chaplain. Used by permission..

How Is Being a Chaplain
Different from Being a Pastor?

> In the hospital, the chaplain is in a different context. Instead of chancels and pulpits, one is at bedsides, in recovery, and in emergency rooms, spending more time reading patients charts than the Scriptures. It is a world in which the chaplain feels little primacy. Certainly in this setting, the chaplain is not treated with the reverence and favor to which one had grown accustomed in the parish. It is a much lonelier world, one without mutual covenants and support of a worshipping community. In a setting where tasks are so carefully delineated and precisely measured, the chaplain feels out of place.[1]

This is how one chaplain would describe the differences in being a chaplain from being a pastor. Many pastors might justifiably quibble with the idea that pastors feel a sense of "reverence and respect" from parish members, but one can still see the chaplain's point. Chaplains are asked to provide crisis ministry to patients whom they met only minutes ago, and without knowing most of the information that such ministry commands. Their role becomes, then, somewhat more passive—more facilitation than prescription. The work that chaplains do is not quantifiable nor can it be attractively and impressively displayed in a computer presentation of the hospital's effectiveness.

Some chaplains even feel rejected by parish ministers. There is a (sometimes justifiable) prejudice that chaplains have left church and "faith talk" for psychology and "therapeutic psychobabble." Some pastors do not understand or appreciate that a chaplain is trained to respond clinically to a patient's condition, and that the chaplain may not feel the same sense of outrage or grief that the minister feels. In some cases, the difference in educational level between the chaplain and the pastor fosters unspoken distrust.

Patients, too, sometimes distrust chaplains. Perhaps they distrust and are prejudiced against all clergy, and the chaplain is lumped in with "all those hypocritical preachers." On the other hand, they may have been taught by the sermons of their own clergy to distrust and doubt the orthodoxy of all clergy outside their personal faith tradition, in which case the chaplain may be regarded as "heathen." You can support the work of your local chaplain by inviting her (or him) to lead in your worship services or to speak at a church gathering.

Teach your congregation to appreciate your hospital chaplains. Ask your patients if they have been visited by a chaplain, and then speak positively of the chaplain's ministry. Encourage the patient to call on a chaplain if they have a question or "need a second opinion." Volunteer to attend training and then to "hold the chaplain's beeper" so that he or she can enjoy a weekend off with family or friends, if this is allowed by the local hospital. Offer to buy the chaplain a cup of coffee or a soft drink, and sit down for a friendly conversation. Offer to conduct worship services in the hospital chapel for ambulatory patients, families, and staff, especially on holidays such as Thanksgiving, Christmas, and Easter. Encourage the church family to provide "goodies" for the on-call hospital chaplains during these holidays. Use your own sanctified imagination to find creative and supportive ways to honor your hospital chaplains!

When Should You Call on the Hospital Chaplain?

This can be a very long list, but remember that the hospital chaplain must work with many ministers and patients. Be respectful of the chaplain's time. Keeping things simple, there are three times when you should call on the chaplain:

1. When you need information about a patient or access to a patient.
2. When you don't know how to minister to a patient.
3. When you need the support of a trained, professional colleague in ministry.

A chaplain has access to the Emergency Room, Intensive Care Unit, Cardiac Care Unit, and Maternity Unit at times when you may not, so the chaplain may be able to help you comfort a fearful family. The chaplain may also be willing to check with the medical staff in the unit while you wait with the family. Keep in mind that there are confidentiality guidelines with which he may need to conform.

A chaplain also has training in medical terms and procedures that is superior to yours, so contact a chaplain if you, a patient, or a patient's family is unclear about the patient's treatment or condition. Again, this is for familiarity only—a chaplain does not diagnose illnesses.

A second time to contact the chaplain is whenever you simply do not know how to minister to a family. If you are relatively new to pastoral ministry, the chaplain can be of enormous help. Even if you are a well-seasoned minister, you may find yourself in an unfamiliar circumstance, and in this case, too, a chaplain can give guidance.

Asking the chaplain to be with you at the time of a death is particularly wise. He will have specific training in dealing with the details of a death, and will free you to comfort and pray with the family. He will know how to contact a funeral home and what to do if the family is still present when the funeral director comes to pick up the deceased.

The support of a hospital chaplain has been most help-ful to me in situations involving the death of an infant or child. I learned from a chaplain that it was good for the grieving parents to hold and kiss a stillborn or deceased infant or child. I learned patience with the grieving and emotion that are a necessary part of such a death, and I learned to let the parents set the tone and the timetable for grieving. I learned that some parents wish to have their infant baptized after death, even if that ritual is not a part of their faith tradition. I learned that the most important and comforting thing a pastor can say to the grieving family of a deceased child is "I will remember your child" or "Your child will not be forgotten." All these things I learned from a hospital chaplain, and I bless him for that.

The third time in which it is particularly helpful to call on the chaplain is when you need the support of a pro-fessional colleague. I have asked the chaplain to accom-pany me when I needed to tell a patient in the psychiatric ward that a loved one had died, and that the patient would not be able to attend the funeral. I have asked for the assistance of the chaplain when I was pres-ent with a physician as the bad news of a terminal diag-nosis was explained. I am quite sure that sometimes the person who most needed the chaplain was me, not the family, but the chaplain never let on that he knew.

One Sunday evening as I was preparing to leave the church office to go to the sanctuary to begin a worship service, a young man came into the office and asked to see a pastor. I responded that I was a pastor and won-dered aloud if the problem might not wait until after the worship service. He assured me that the problem would not wait and that he intended to kill himself in the next few minutes. In response to my worried question, he responded that yes, he did have a weapon and he intended to use it on himself. He said that he would accept help not to commit suicide if I could find it for him quickly. He said that he would kill himself on the spot if he heard police sirens approaching. While I prayed that no one would need the police, fire, or ambulance services in that area anytime soon, I dialed the number of the chaplain at the closest hospital. With the young man sitting across the desk from me, I asked how I could get help for my friend who was feeling suicidal, and who apparently had a gun with him, and who didn't care to visit with the police just then. At the chaplain's direction, I invited the young man to ride with me in my vehicle to the emergency room of the hospital. The hospital staff, who were aware of the situation, did a physical exam on the young man, which seemed to quiet him and he agreed to a ride in an ambulance to the regional mental health center thirty miles away. Later that evening, when I had depressurized and was ready for bed, I remembered to thank the hospital chaplain for his help. For some reason, I had forgotten to do so at the time.

What to Do When Hospice Is Used

Although the focus of this book is the hospital visit, in some cases, hospice care is a valid adjunct to hospital care. Hospice care involves a team-oriented approach of expert medical care, pain management, and emotional and spiritual support expressly tailored to the terminally ill patient's wishes. Emotional and spiritual support are also extended to the family and loved ones. Generally, this care is provided in the patient's home or in a home-like setting operated by a hospice program.

Hospice seeks to address not only physical pain, but also emotional, social, and spiritual pain to achieve the "best possible quality of life for patients and their families." To better serve individuals who have advanced illness or are terminally ill and their families, many hospice programs encourage access to care earlier in the illness or disease process. Healthcare professionals who specialize in hospice work closely with staff and volunteers to address all the symptoms of illness, with the aim of promoting comfort and dignity.

How does the pastor relate to hospice care? In my experience, hospice has welcomed my involvement and actively sought my advice and presence as decisions about the course of treatment were made. In most cases, hospice encouraged pastoral care and kept me informed of opportunities when I needed to be present.

Perhaps a short encouragement is in order here. One hospice nurse told me that her greatest disappointment with pastors was their inability to speak honestly and openly about death. She said that some pastors even avoided making hospice visits, using excuses like "I would rather remember him the way he was." What this actually reveals is an intense discomfort with the fact of death, and an immature way of coping. Don't let this happen to you! Get help if you need it, but be there when your parishioners need you most.

Note

1. Lawrence E. Holst, "The Hospital Chaplain: Between Worlds," in Lawrence E. Holst, ed., *Hospital Ministry: The Role of the Chaplain Today* (New York: Crossroad, 1985), p. 13.

CHAPTER SIX

The Pastor as Patient: Relating to Our Own Woundedness

The nurse from the Critical Care Unit called about 11:00 A.M. and asked me to come to the hospital in my role as volunteer chaplain. A family there needed support, and she asked if I could come quickly. I agreed and arrived at the hospital less than ten minutes later. When I entered the CCU, what I saw stopped me cold. A five-year-old boy lay on the bed, connected by tubes to every machine available. The nurse explained to me that the child had come to the hospital with an advanced case of meningitis, and his death was only a matter of time. I asked her to take me to the family, where I listened as they poured out their grief and pain and asked that I pray with them and for them. In a matter of minutes, the physician came to the waiting room to tell them that despite the best efforts of the medical staff, the son had died. It felt to me as if all the air had been sucked out of the room, and then there was an explosion of wailing, crying, and screaming. The doctor, nurses, and I each sat with a grieving person until the initial storm passed. When the mother regained her composure, she asked to be taken to her son so that she could hold him. A compassionate nurse had already disconnected and removed all the tubes from his body, and I was left with the family as they held their lost son, and stroked his hair and kissed his cheeks. After their immediate grief spent itself, I talked with them and asked if I could contact a funeral home for them. The family gave me instructions, and before they left, I prayed with them, walked them to their cars, came inside to contact the funeral home, and then left to go back to the church. The entire experience lasted only about two hours, and yet every detail seems fresh in my mind. This was not the first time that I had cared for a family after a death, but this experience was by far the most traumatic I had yet experienced, for the boy who died looked like my own blond-haired five-year-old son.

Prior to this experience, I looked forward to each call to serve as volunteer chaplain at the hospital. I felt competent to serve (although I wasn't really) and thought I could render a necessary and valuable service to the patients and families that I served. I was not so anxious to answer such calls for a period of time after the death of the little blond-haired boy, for anxieties about the health of my own children weighed heavily on me. Time and maturity heal, but the emotional impact of that day and my own unreadiness to deal with my feelings left a long-term wound.

The Wounds We All Endure

The description of the pastor as "wounded healer" comes from the marvelous book of the same name by Henri Nouwen. The thesis of that book, that all clergy are both the wounded and the agents of healing, has influenced many since its publication in 1972. Unfortunately, many pastors overemphasized the psychological insights of Nouwen's work and the concept of "woundedness" at the cost of his insistence on the importance of the healing power of the grace of God. Whatever the damage done, the image is still powerful.

Nouwen quotes the following passage from the Talmud, taken from the tractate Sanhedrin, as a paradigm for the pastor who is both wounded and a healer.

> Rabbi Yoshual ben Levi came upon Elijah the prophet while he was standing at the entrance of Rabbi Simeron ben Yohai's cave. . . . He asked Elijah, "When will the Messiah come?" Elijah replied, "Go and ask him yourself."
>   "Where is he?"
>   "Sitting at the gates of the city."
>   "How shall I know him?"
>   "He is sitting among the poor covered with wounds. The others unbind all their wounds at the same time and then bind them up again. But he unbinds one at a time and binds it up again, saying to himself, 'Perhaps I shall be needed: if so I must always be ready so as not to delay for a moment." [1]

Nouwen writes that this is the situation of the contemporary pastor, who is both wounded minister and a healing minister. As a "healing minister," the pastor is one who both experiences healing and offers the possibility of healing to others.

When you visit the hospital, you will never know ahead of time what you will encounter. You may be surprised, shocked, embarrassed, embraced, or blessed, but you will take with you your unique, God-given personality, family history, and experience. You are, and will remain, a "wounded healer." How well you minister to others will depend largely on how well you have come to terms with your own past, personality, sins, strengths, gifts, and successes. The purpose of this chapter is to suggest ways in which you can become more aware both of your woundedness and of your being healed.

When we answer the call to become a pastor, we bring with us the *wounds of our childhood and our past*. Each person carries with him these experiences, and they shape and influence the behavior of the pastor as an adult. These experiences can be either a source of strength or the cause of troubles and sadness in adult life, depending on whether they are acknowledged and accepted or denied and repressed. Psychotherapist Thomas Maeder noted in an article in the *Atlantic Monthly* that the "helping professions," particularly psychotherapy and the ministry, "appear to attract more than their share of the emotionally unstable." He further refers to studies that "suggest a high incidence of family problems and narcissistic disorders, and a host of other problems involving interpersonal relations and self-esteem."[2] While I do not share Maeder's apparent pessimism regarding pastors, those who cannot form and maintain positive interpersonal relationships do not tend to be either fulfilled or successful in their ministries. Pastors who struggle with fears regarding illness, death, or intimacy will have a particularly difficult time with hospital visitation, and will likely seek to avoid it or delegate this responsibility to others.

Pastors are particularly at risk for being *wounded by the unreasonable expectations of ministry*. Often the expectations that our congregations hold for us are informal or even unwritten and uncommunicated. Pastors are expected to be not only above reproach, but also above gossip. I know of one pastor whose ministry to a church was compromised because his parishioners thought that his running shorts were too short for dignified and appropriate pastoral wear, evening for running, and this was during the summertime in Texas!

Wayne Oates confronts the possibility of being hurt in ministry in a direct manner when he writes: "The ever-present fact of gossip and slander in a community hovers like humidity over the face-to-face ministry of a pastor. You may be unaware of it, but you are never free of its influence."[3] John Killinger, when he had returned to the parish ministry after teaching homiletics in a seminary, wrote about a telephone call that his wife took. One dear lady called to say that another lady, not so well intentioned, was bad-mouthing the pastor because he had not visited her mother. Actually, he had visited the woman's mother, but she was too senile to remember the visit; so don't forget to leave those business cards! His wife replied sweetly to the nice lady who called: "Tell her to phone me, there are two things that I would like say to her." "Oh?" replied the voice on the line. "Yes," said his wife. "First, John is not God, and, second, stuff it!"[4]

Although most pastors' spouses (or pastors themselves) will never have the opportunity for such a direct response to the sometimes unwarranted expectations of churches, we all must live with their existence. Pastors are screens onto which are projected people's hang-ups and their legitimate expectations.[5] Hospital visitation is one of the chief sources of contention between pastors and congregations, and conflict generally is based on the miscommunication illustrated by Killinger's story.

In most contemporary churches, a pastor's effectiveness is judged by the numbers of new members the church enlists, by the growth in the church's budget and its gifts to the denomination, or by how well the members of the congregation like him or her. Many pastors, therefore, begin to judge themselves on the basis of a ministerial beauty pageant, in which the numbers for congeniality, attractiveness, poise, and popularity are tabulated and the winner announced on the public stage of approval ratings. The results are frequently devastating for the pastor, for she begins to regard each task for its value in increasing her approval rating, and hospital visitation, particularly for peripheral members of the congregation, comes up a poor alternative to more efficient means of influencing members. Though it may take some time, the pastor begins to suffer the *wounds of a lack of self-awareness.*

The most serious of these wounds is a loss of caring for others. As Mayerhoff observes: "I cannot be fully present for the other if I am more concerned about how I appear to other people than I am with seeing and responding to its needs."[6] All ministries of the pastor suffer when this occurs, but none like that of hospital visitation, which does take considerable time and energy.

Some pastors are not taught to recognize and cope with the powerful impact that emotions can have on a person's spiritual and emotional health. Like some other professionals, some pastors excel in their academic pursuits at the cost of developing the self-awareness and emotional maturity of a balanced adult, and the outcome for these individuals is the unwelcome need for developing a healthy emotional life while also learning to be an effective pastor. For these pastors, the emotions present in hospital visitation go unrecognized and unacknowledged until a personal crisis develops, and the pastor is wounded by his inability to appropriately acknowledge his own grief.

The inability of the emotionally and spiritually immature pastor to deal with the pressures, expectations, and trauma of ministry, especially hospital visitation, can cause the pastor to know the pain of *self-inflicted wounds* in ministry. These might include such behaviors as:

- trying to replace God in relationships with patients and families;
- practicing medicine by giving patients and families unwarranted advice;
- promising more than can be delivered;
- disrupting relationships in her own family by "taking her problems home with her";

- talking too much, and listening too little;
- avoiding hospital visitation if possible;
- using your pastoral position of authority to meet your own emotional needs.

When you recognize these behaviors in yourself, or in a close friend, it is time to confront the problem directly. Pastors engage in these behaviors as a warning to others that they are in emotional and spiritual pain and need help in resolving their internal conflicts.

The High Cost of Failure

For too many pastors, the cost of the failure to cope with the emotional burden of the ministry of hospital visitation is *repression*. If you pretend that you do not feel the pain and suffering of your parishioners, you soon fail to feel your own pain or even your legitimate concern for yourself and your family. The inability of a pastor to mourn, either privately or publicly, the loss and pain of caring for his flock leads to emotional depression and spiritual deadness, robbing the pastor, her family, and her church of the spiritual vitality and involvement that they have a right to want and to expect. As Killinger observed:

> The shame is that we become robots—mechanical people, going through the motions of ministry. The clerical mask is there—by the sickbed, in the counseling session, behind the pulpit, by the graveside—but the face behind it grows more and more passionless, more and more anonymous. Work, because it is demanding and relentless, becomes routine. The edges of personhood are ground off. We come to the dinner table and stare, as the discussion ebbs and flows around us. Our children grow up and we wonder when it happened. Our wives or husbands grow old alone, companionless as herons in the twilight.[7]

Other pastors take the opposite route, substituting an increasingly hollow demand for authority in their relationships with their parishioners, leaving themselves open to a form of *idolatry*. Since we symbolize the presence of God for many people, and we are regarded by some as possessing a source of wisdom and power divine in its origin, pastors sometimes begin to confuse their role as God's representative with the desire to supplant God in the life of their parishioners. Wayne Oates quotes Otto Rank in describing the desire of every person who turns to the minister for help as the tendency to make of the pastor a god, with the unconscious need to idolize and to desecrate him or her at the same time. This is what Rank called the "unreal need for a god in human form."[8]

Eugene Peterson captures precisely the allure of this temptation:

> As a counselor, the pastor is secularized into functioning away from being a friend in Christ to functioning as a substitute for God, which is, in effect, an act of idolatry. It is an extremely difficult process to resist, for who does not like being treated as a god? ... Persons look for experts to solve their problems for them so that they will not have to acquire competence to live authentically and responsibly. They are used to deferring to experts in every other area of life—why not here?[9]

The obvious problem with this approach is, of course, that sooner or later the piper must be paid and the pastor undergoes the flip side of the adoration that she has received, which is the desecration that Rank describes. In this instance, the pastor receives criticism that is as unfair and undeserved as the adulation that she received. Eventually she is forced to leave that church, and the pain of that experience is added to the many others that are repressed.

Pastors understandably tire of the cycle of being idolized and desecrated, and as a result, there are pastors who continue to serve God even though they are disillusioned by the experience. In the words of Thomas Maeder: "These people are pathological givers. . . . They have given so much that they finally run out of spiritual and nervous energy, and what remains is the underlying resentment. You find a great deal of resentment and sourness among the clergy."[10]

What results is that some pastors simply choose to react in a passive-aggressive manner and conclude that "if no one will help me deal with my pain, then I will not help anyone else deal with theirs." This is not only an immature and ineffective means of confronting one's own emotional and spiritual bankruptcy, but it will always lead to serious problems with the congregation, sometimes resulting in termination. I am an expert on this situation, for I have experienced it at firsthand.

My own inability to deal with the emotional trauma of ministry, including hospital visitation, in conjunction with the serious illness of one of my children, gradually led me to the experience of resenting what I perceived to be the obligation of hospital visitation and of avoiding the pain that I was afraid that I would have to experience in that visitation. Because I had never learned to respond appropriately to emotional trauma, I repressed the fear that my emotions would overcome and overwhelm me. Frederick Buechner expressed with greater truth than I can manage his experience of living through the same experience with his child: "I had virtually given up doing anything in the way of feeding myself humanly. To be at peace is to have peace inside yourself more or less in spite of what is going on outside yourself. In that sense I had no peace at all."[11]

At the end of this sad journey, I failed miserably to provide the support that one family needed and deserved. By God's grace, I did find the strength and wisdom to confront my own sinfulness and failure, to visit the family, to confess my sin and to seek forgiveness, and to seek restoration with them. Though there was real and permanent damage, there was also some measure of redemption in the experience. The irony, of course, is that this happened while I was writing this book.

The Source of Our Healing

Is God. There is no need to complicate this issue. God is the source of our healing, through the willing sacrifice of the obedient Son, and the divine direction of the Holy Spirit. The first step, obviously, is that we must want and willingly accept the grace of God in our lives. The writer of the wisdom saying in Proverbs 18:14 captures the despair of the wounded: "A man's spirit sustains him in sickness, but a crushed spirit who can bear?" (NIV). God's response to us even today is that of God to the apostle Paul, "My grace is sufficient for you, for my power is made perfect in weakness" (2 Cor. 12:9 NIV). Our testimony is that even our most grievous sin is God's opportunity for redemption and grace: "That is why, for Christ's sake, I delight in weaknesses, in insults, in hardships, in persecutions, in difficulties. For when I am weak, then I am strong" (2 Cor. 12:10 NIV). We are wounded by our own sinful choices, and by the sinful actions of others. We are healed by the sacrificial love shown to us by Christ: "For to be sure, he was crucified in weakness, yet he lives by God's power. Likewise, we are weak in him, yet by God's power we will live with him to serve you" (2 Cor. 13:4 NIV).

This is my testimony to God's healing and forgiving grace. It is in no way more remarkable than that of any other person; but to me it seems more remarkable, more miraculous, more full of the stuff of God than I have gift to communicate. What does this have to do with hospital visitation? Both nothing and everything, for it renewed my desire to serve God and my ability to do so. It is my access to both God and others. It is my shame and my glory. It is God's good work in me: "And I am sure that God, who began the good work within you, will continue his work until it is finally finished on that day when Christ Jesus comes back again" (Phil. 1:6 NLT).

The "Quick-Start Page"

All computer software packages have "quick-start pages" for those who are so eager to begin that they do not wish to read the entire instruction book. For those who cannot bear to read the rest of the story before they know how the story turns out, here is a summary of the lessons of this book:

1. Never forget that your presence conveys the presence of God to those whom you visit. Prepare yourself to be an effective hospital visitor by learning the basics of visitation.
2. Bring the hope of Christ's healing and presence to each patient that you visit.
3. Like the Holy Spirit, comfort the family of the patient with your prayers. Make the ministry of the Holy Spirit your model in caring for hurting families.
4. Shepherd your congregation as Christ shepherded his disciples, both teaching and discipling them in Christian growth.
5. Trust and depend on the hospital chaplain, your colleague in ministry. Learn from her, for she has much to teach you.

6. Take care of yourself. Learn to recognize your own woundedness, and to seek the healing of God in your life and ministry.

As Wayne Oates, to whom this author is obviously greatly indebted, quotes his own mentor, Ray Petry, professor of church history at the Duke Divinity School: "Ailing physicians are we all, students. But we *will do*, for God has chosen us!"[12]

Notes

1. Henri Nouwen, *The Wounded Healer* (New York: Doubleday, 1972), pp. 81-82.
2. Thomas Maeder, "Wounded Healers," *Atlantic Monthly*, January 1989, p. 37.
3. Wayne E. Oates, *The Christian Pastor,* third edition, revised (Philadelphia: Westminster Press, 1982), p. 101.
4. John Killinger, *Christ in the Seasons of Ministry* (Waco, Tex.: Word, 1981), p. 44.
5. Alan Jones, *Sacrifice and Delight: Spirituality for Ministry* (New York: HarperCollins, 1992), p. 19.
6. Milton Mayerhoff, *On Caring* (New York: HarperCollins, 1971), p. 26.
7. Killinger, *Christ in the Seasons of Ministry,* p. 47.
8. Oates, *The Christian Pastor,* p. 72.
9. Eugene Peterson, *Five Smooth Stones for Pastoral Work* (Grand Rapids: Eerdmans, 1992), p. 91.
10. Maeder, "Wounded Healers," p. 42.
11. Frederick Buechner, *Telling Secrets* (New York: Harper Collins, 1991), p. 25.
12. Wayne E. Oates, *The Presence of God in Pastoral Counseling* (Waco, Tex.: Word, 1986), p. 186.

Appendix

If you serve as pastor in a faith tradition which offers you a prayerbook as a resource for hospital visitation, then you are fortunate indeed. For those pastors who do not have access to such a resource, or for those who may wish to add other prayers to their ministry, I offer the following as a starting point for your own use.

Prayers for the Hospital

For a Person Who Has Died

Dear Jesus, our resurrection and our life,
Please give rest to (name) who, died believing in you. Return (his) soul to you and your care. Give (him) the dawn of an eternal life with you, and protect (him)from the sting of death. Bless this family with your shepherding presence as they must walk through the valley of the shadow of death. Comfort them, and keep them from despair with the hope of your resurrection. In the name of the conqueror of death we pray, Amen.

For a Family Facing an Uncertain Outcome

O God of all comfort and hope,
I bring my friends to you in prayer, holding them up to

your throne that they may know the comfort of your presence in their hearts and lives. My love for them, poured out by your Holy Spirit into my heart, prompts me to intercede for them in their fears and their hopes. Send healing to their loved one, (name), and to them. If my prayer does not deserve to be answered, then love them for their own sakes and guide them to love you, whose care for them is beyond comprehension. Grant them the bounty of your grace for them not according to my prayers but out of your infinite love and gracious care. I offer this prayer as a child seeks out her parents for comfort. In the hope of your grace we pray, Amen.

For a Person Seeking Understanding

Lord, since only you can bring understanding to our faith through the Holy Spirit, I ask that you grant the blessing of understanding to my (brother, name). He is perplexed and disheartened by the turns that (his) life has taken, and discomforted by the uncertainty of the future. Allow (him) to know the freedom that (he) has in you, freedom so great that (he) may even question you as Jesus did, asking "My God, my God, why have you forsaken me?" Grant (him) a clear understanding of how (he) might know you, and knowing you grow in (his) trust of you. Above all, grant to (him) the peace that you have promised for (his) life, a peace that surpasses all of (his) need to understand your will for (him). I ask this prayer in the name of Jesus, who trusted you, and won our victory forever. Amen.

A Bedside Prayer

Be (his) light through the darkness that surrounds (him). Be (his) guide through the testing that (he) is enduring. Guard (him) from whatever would attack (his) soul, and sustain (his) relationship of loving trust with you. Give (him) rest so that (he) might heal and be made whole, in spirit as well as in body. Guide the hands and enlighten the minds of those who care for (his) body, that they may exercise to the best of their ability the gifts of healing which you have granted to them. Gladden (his) heart with your peace, for (his) sake and for (his) comfort. In the healing name of Jesus I ask this. Amen.

For a Person Facing Surgery (When the Family Is Also Present)

Jesus, whose touch healed the sick and restored the sight of the blind, we ask that you be with (name), who is about to undergo surgery. We trust in you, for you can heal. We hope in you, for you will guide the hands of the doctors and nurses who will perform this surgery. We rest in you, who can give strength for recovery and for waiting. We need you, for our faith is tested in our fears and anxieties. Grant sucess to this surgery, and a swift return to health for our loved one. Grant the comfort of your presence in the hearts of this family as they wait for the surgery to be completed. Calm their souls as you calmed the seas, with your presence and your strength. We ask this prayer in the name of Jesus. Amen.

At the Death of a Child

Holy God,
We offer up to you the life of this little one, (name). Her life was so brief, yet (she) brought so much joy to her parents and family. Comfort us with the memory that you gathered little children around you, and loved them. So we ask that you gather little (name) to you in heaven, and that S(he) may not know pain or sorrow, but rather that S(he) might live in your presence now and forever.

Help these young parents to trust that their child, (name), is even now in your care. I ask you Lord to fulfill your promise to them to comfort them as a mother would comfort her own children. Give them the strength and courage to grieve as they must, and grant them a sense of your presence in each step on the way.

If you feel comfortable in doing so, add:

Some day, when it is your will, I ask that you might bless them with reunion with each other as a blessing of heaven. Amen.

For a Person Who Wishes to Accept Her Own Death, and to Make Peace with Her Own Mortality

Lord Jesus Christ, who is the source of health for the living and the promise of eternal life to the dying, I ask you to bless my (sister) in (her) suffering. If your will for (her) is that (she) continue to live in this world, then heal (her) and restore (her) to useful life. If your will for (he)R is that (she) live with you in heaven forever, then give (her) the strength and wisdom to lay aside (her) mortal body, that (she) may be clothed in the glory of (her) resurrection body. For (her) sake I ask that whatever your will for (her), that you would relieve (her) of pain and bring meaning to (her) suffering, so that (she) may rest peacefully. In the name of Jesus, who is both our life and our resurrection. Amen.

For a Person in a Mental Hospital, or Who Is Suffering from a Mental Illness

O Holy Spirit, who can see deeply into the hearts and minds of every person, I pray that you might penetrate deeply into the mind and soul of (name). Bring (her) cleansing, healing, health, and wholeness of body and mind. Grant the blesxsings of your promise in Psalm 91, and gather (her) under your wing, granting (her) the comfort that only you can give. I ask this in the name of Jesus, who cast out evil and healed human minds. Amen.

For a Person Who Is Depressed

I entreat you, Lord, who is the source of abundant life, to restore the spirit of my (brother) (name) who is suffering from depression, which robs (him) of the joy of living and makes even the most important things of life seem impossibly difficult to do. Help (him) to trust that you will care for (him) even when this seems most impossible. Restore hope to (his) life, the hope that whatever tomorrow brings will not overcome (him). Calm (his) anxieties as you once calmed the seas, and be the light in (his) life. As you overcame depression in the lives of Jonah and of Elisha, I ask now that you heal (name) of this condition. Amen.

For a Person Who Is in a Comatose Condition or Who Suffers from Alzheimer's Disease

Our Father in Heaven and in our hearts,
There are so many things that we long to say to (name), and to know that (she) has heard us. We want to tell (her) of our love and of our resolve to do our best by (her). We long to feel close to (her), and to hear (her) voice again. If this is your will, Lord, grant (her) back (her) life, that (she) may again love intentionally and laugh at the joy of living. It pains us to say this, Holy God, but our lives are filled more with hell than with heaven. For (her) sake, for our sakes, and for your sake please bring meaning, understanding, and peace to our lives. Amen.

After the Birth of a Child

I lift this newborn child up to you,
who formed (her) in (her) mother's womb,
Who brought (her) safely into this world,
Who will be (her) guardian and guide throughout (her) life.
Let (her) learn about your love for (her) as a child.
Let (her) learn the joy of following you as a young person.
Let (her) serve you as an adult, granting (her) a long life in which to praise you.
Prepare (her) for life in heaven with you.
Equip these young parents with your wisdom. Give them strength to protect (her). Give her faith to raise (her) to know you. Give them courage to do what is best for (her).
In the name of Jesus, who loved little children, I ask this prayer. Amen.

For the Successful Completion of a Surgery

We thank you, Lord, for the successful surgery of our (brother), (name). Thank you for guiding the hands and directing the thoughts of (his) doctors and nurses. Now mend (his) body, and grant (him) a quick and successful recovery. Bless (him) with strength to wait for (his) healing to be complete. Encourage (him) with the will to persevere through the pain of (his) recovery. Strengthen (his) spirit on days when progress seems small and time creeps by. Lead (him) to grow in trust and in dependence on you. We praise you for the success of this surgery. Amen.

For a Person Who Has Died Suddenly

O God, we are in shock, and we do not know what to do. (name) has been torn from our lives, and the pain of (his) loss seems too much to bear right now. He died before we could say all that (he) meant to us, and we are heartbroken that we will never again be able to speak to (him), and to be with (him). We pray, O God, that you will be merciful to (him) and that (he) might be in heaven with you. We ask that someday we might be reunited with (him) in heaven. Help us to remember that you are the Lord of this life, and of the life to come, and that you care for us in both this life and in life eternal. Comfort us with the hope that you are the resurrection and the life, and that you are a very present help in times of trouble. Bless us with your grace, for we have no other source of strength than you. Amen.